T0339790

IN THE HEAT OF SHADOWS

South African Poetry 1996-2013

In the Heat of Shadows

South African Poetry 1996-2013

Edited by
Denis Hirson

deepsouth

ISBN: 978-0-9870282-3-5
ebook ISBN: 978-1-928476-19-1

Deep South
contact@deepsouth.co.za
www.deepsouth.co.za

Distributed in South Africa by
University of KwaZulu-Natal Press
www.ukznpress.co.za

Distributed worldwide by
African Books Collective
PO Box 721, Oxford, OX1 9EN, UK
www.africanbookscollective.com/publishers/deep-south

Cover art: Maja Maljevic, *Nirox Diaries* 7 (Oil on canvas)
Text and cover design: Liz Gowans

The publication of this book is a legacy project of
the South Africa-France Seasons 2012 & 2013.
www.france-southafrica.com

Contents

INTRODUCTION

ANYONE who followed the development of South African poetry through the darkest of the apartheid years, and was aware of its constantly recurring themes of guilt and victimization, rage and denial, identity and dispossession, might be surprised by its current reach and range.

South African poets today find themselves writing in the midst of uneasy political transformation, some of it neither planned nor hoped for, while spinning outwards from the casing of isolation to join the bustle and complexity of the turning world. Their work is charged with restlessness, bursting with diversity. Gone is the intense inward focus required to deal with a situation of systematic oppression, though awareness of that time continues to surface sharply. Gone is the overriding, enclosing effort of concentration on a single predicament. Instead, the reader will discover outward reaching poems that record movement through time and space, experiments in language and translation, alongside enduring touchstones such as love and loss, memory and acts of witnessing. Faced with this rich array of work, I have made out of it a collage of many dimensions, rather than doggedly trying to pursue specific themes or approaches.

A number of the poets whose work is represented here came to the fore between the late 1980's and the mid-1990's, at a time when the country was achingly alive with dreams of change. I believe much of today's dynamic in South African poetry can be traced back to that period. Robert Berold, who edited the magazine *New Coin* between 1989 and 1999 and transformed it into a unique seismograph of the times, appropriately named the anthology he sifted from those years *It All Begins*, after a poem by Mxolisi Nyezwa which is reproduced here. This poem might well be referring to the Truth and Reconciliation Commission of 1996-1998: "It all begins with one statement,/ with the scratch of one pen. / it begins with the smell of death dying/ with people of all sizes in every epoch/ shouting from the grave".

Antjie Krog, in the extract from "Country of grief and grace" which opens this anthology, believes the identity of the entire country widened as a result of the Commission, since it allowed for the emergence of hidden, unspeakable apartheid-era stories, spoken by voices "baptised in syllables of blood and belonging". One section of her poem concludes with the line "This country belongs to the voices who live in it", and it is bearing in mind this perception of the conflictual emergence of multiple voices that I have chosen 1996 as the starting point for *In the Heat of Shadows*.

A political conversation runs through these pages, from Krog's overture, through Karen Press's reference to one ex-political prisoner who came before the Commission ("Do you love yourself like this") to Ingrid de Kok's interrogations concerning that same man's torturer ("What kind of man?"). The conversation takes on a broader tone of disenchantment in Vonani Bila's "In the name of Amandla", Rustum Kozain's "Comrades", Kelwyn Sole's "This is not autumn" and Jim Pascual Agustin's "People who live with lions", all published in the years following Mandela's resignation from power, touching in one way or another on the "vast regions of my country/ rolled around their ulcer and their pain" as Kozain puts it in "Death".

More specifically, in "Our president", Rosamund Stanford expresses the unease and distrust surrounding Jacob Zuma today, while Vonani Bila in "Baba Mandela" and Karen Press in the extract from "Praise poem: I saw you coming towards me" express despair at Mandela's political actions as a retired old man. I should add that I have resisted the temptation to include here any of the rising number of poems written on Mandela's death, most of them shying away from acceptance of his human fallibility and revealing instead a need to elevate him to the level of a demigod; a need perhaps equal and opposite to the depths of difficulty prevailing in the country he once led. Not that the political vision suggested in this anthology is unequivocally negative. Keorapetse Kgositsile (quoting Abdellatif Laabi) remounts "the curve of evil times/ to unearth my anchored memory" ("Renaissance"), while Jeremy Cronin maintains a sense of hope despite the "slant-wise" ironies of "End of the century – which is why wipers".

The poems I have mentioned show the poet as pulse-taker, messenger and critic, a role which was perceived to be fundamental at the time of apartheid when so many political voices were gagged. This role belongs to a tradition stretching back long before 1948 to poets as diverse as Thomas Pringle, SEK Mqhayi, NP van Wyk Louw and generation upon generation of iimbongi who have acted as intermediaries between the people and their leaders.

Most contributors to *In the Heat of Shadows* who have taken on such a role today make it implicitly or explicitly clear that those they wish to address have disappointed them. The high hopes for post-apartheid South Africa have not been met, and those they address are being held at least partly responsible. "Did you imagine/ it would turn out like this?" asks Karen Press of the tortured prisoner turned corrupt MP, ending her poem with the lightly flicked whiplash of praise: "You were so beautiful then" ("Do you love yourself like this"). Such cross-examination, its underlying sense of betrayal, spiked with reminders of the shared dream and complicity with the past, injects the anthology with a singularly acid atmosphere.

This is only sharpened by those poems recording the implosive unease and violence pervading people's intimate existence, as in Kelwyn Sole's "I live in a house", Finuala Dowling's "To the doctor who treated the raped baby and who felt such despair" and the work included here by Mxolisi Nyezwa, David wa Maahlamela, Nathan Trantraal and Ronelda Kamfer. Yet none of these poets takes on the voice of the victim so commonly expressed under apartheid. "I refuse to be anyone's spanner or hammer", affirms Maahlamela in "Autobiography". "I'm not crying over that Apartheid kak" says Ronelda Kamfer in "Retelling 2", going on to berate her people for not seeking out their own story but rather reproducing a caricature invented for them. If the language is sometimes purposefully crude, this only serves to fuel more intensely the energies needed to move beyond the discourse of dependence, to a point where the poem becomes part of the dialogue between poet and community.

Which is not to say that the memory of apartheid has faded, or that its pain is less active than before. Rustum Kozain says of his memory of first love that "it hurt me into poetry/ like a country would/ like a country does", and later, "Apartheid hurt us [. . .] beyond the weal of reparations" ("Memory 1"). Gabeba Baderoon looks at a photograph of her mother as a medical student and is reminded of her being obliged to leave the autopsy room because there would be "the uncovering and cutting of white skin" ("I forget to look"). In both cases, the political and the personal mix and crystallize to salt in wounds that are still open.

Memory, stretching back to childhood and the loss of a loved one, marks the work of several poets including Vonani Bila, Gert Vlok Nel, Rustum Kozain, Gabeba Baderoon, Petra Müller, Isobel Dixon, Finuala Dowling, Joan Metelerkamp and myself, just as it is implicit in the homesickness of Toni Stuart's "Ma, I'm comin' home". For a number of poets, there is also a further dimension to memory: as the door to the past is opened, the ancestors enter. These may be historical ancestors as in Rosamund Stanford's stern and wilful "Forefathers"; more often here they are the shades, the presence of the dead who may counsel the living and see to their wellbeing. This is the case when it comes to the ritual voice of imbongi Bulelani Zantsi, as also to the work of Bongekile Mbanjwa, for whom the living will be "called to account" by them ("Lock and key"). Ancestors emerge in one way or another in poems by David wa Maahlamela and Joan Metelerkamp (whose funeral canoe, in "Deliver her from the depths", implicitly transports the dead to the realm of the ancestors). The full extent of their presence in accompanying daily life is clearly rendered in Vonani Bila's "Ancestral wealth", which opens with the lines "Under these tall thorn umbrella trees/ My ancestors dwell".

The ancestral theme is part of a second conversation which stretches through this anthology, extending a poem such as "Ancestral wealth" well beyond the scope of calendar time and tangible space, admitting the mediation of the dead among the living, taking the vision of the world to the edge of myth, as in Bila's lines "My ancestors rise like elephants/ At the break of dawn/To drink water/ From the mountain's fountain". Naming an entire "pageantry" of ancestors is an integral part

16

of the affirmation of deep identity, as in the opening incantation of Khadija Tracey Heeger's "I am". The energies gathered in such poems, as in others including Kamfer's "Retelling 2", are all the greater since these are poets reclaiming a history and sense of ancestry denied for centuries by successive white regimes.

There are also other ways in which time opens outwards across these pages. There is the historical time of Mongane Wally Serote's "Freedom, lament and song", Jeremy Cronin's "End of the century – which is why wipers" and Ari Sitas's "Slave trades"; the prehistoric time of Marlene van Niekerk's "Rock painting", the mythical time of Petra Müller's "Night crossing II". This expansion is coupled with a multiplicity of references to places outside South Africa, among them China, the United Kingdom, Afghanistan, Canada, France, North Africa, Saint Helena, Rimbaud's Abyssinia, Hitler's Germany and Stalin's USSR.

Not that South African poets in the past failed to recognize the existence of the outside world. There is, though, the impression that, through widening circles of space and time, this poetry is now less hedged in by national borders, more fluidly linked to other times and other places; that Marlene van Niekerk's "wine-brown water of time" ("Rock painting") flows more widely and headily than it might have a few decades back; that a poem such as Karen Press's celebrating "the map that shows how Africans spread across the world to populate it" ("Walking song for Africans abroad") is quintessentially of a country which is no longer a geopolitical island. This impression resonates through Keorapetse Kgositsile's "No boundaries", its affirmation of new freedom perhaps transmuted out of the uprooting of political exile: "I can fly to any place/ or moment fertile with memory/ or create fresh ones without a single boundary".

The outward stretch of South African poetry is accompanied by an equal and opposite movement. The poem, which was in the past so often planted with political signposts, whether published in a magazine of contestation or delivered at a mass rally, can now speak of place in and of itself, without the deliberate, heavily defensive framing of some of the landscape-and-wildlife poetry of previous decades. There is unforced freshness in the natural imagery of the poems by Marlene van Niekerk, in Jim Pascual Agustin's "Chameleon" or Robert Berold's "The water running", very different from the apartheid-laden dispossession of the land that darkens and contracts the wonder of Rustum Kozain's "Kingdom of rain".

At the same time as South African space is freed, so the space of the poem need no longer automatically be taxed for social meaning. The poem can be a place to simply relish the music and visual capacity of words, where "the only truth stands skinned in sound" as Antjie Krog puts it in "Poet becoming", where one might find Jim Pascual Agustin's "little bowls/ brimming with colours/ you have never seen before" ("Missed Fortune"), where Ingrid de Kok enumerates the qualities of her muse ("My muse is a man"). *In the Heat of Shadows* includes experiments which exploit the full self-reflexive, imaginative power of language, intended to transport the reader where only words can go. This is the case for Joan Metelerkamp's "Points on poems" and Katharine Kilalea's "Hennecker's Ditch", where right from the outset words vibrate beyond reason, establishing their own logic: "I stood at the station/ like the pages of a book/ whose words suddenly start to swim". With the opening out of space, there may also be more room for the irresistible if unsettling humour of Kilalea's "Our death", Karen Press's "A cow and a goose" or Finuala Dowling's "Summarizing life".

These, then, are some of the ways in which South African poetry, as selected here, has shifted ground in the past few decades. But perhaps the most important shift recorded in this anthology concerns language itself. The poems here are in the main presented in English, though more than one African language is included in Vonani Bila's "Ancestral wealth". A number of them, by Antjie Krog, Marlene van Niekerk, Gert Vlok Nel, Toni Stuart, Nathan Trantraal and Ronelda Kamfer have been translated from the Afrikaans, in the first two cases by the poets themselves. Isabella Motadinyane has been translated from Sotho and isicamtho (township slang), Bongekile Mbanjwa from Zulu. Bulelani Zantsi's work has metamorphosed from its original oral presentation as a Xhosa praise-poem, to its present written form in English. I also believe I can sometimes hear a French resonance in Ari Sitas's "Slave Trades". The anthology would have been all the poorer had it not been for the many languages involved in its making.

I wonder whether it is really justifiable today to assemble an "anthology of South African poetry" consisting of poems all written originally in the same single language, more particularly English. This tendency was challenged as long ago as 1968, when Jack Cope and Uys Krige brought out their *Penguin Book of South African Verse*. In that volume, poems were divided into sections, by original language. The translations into English were sometimes lacking in inspiration, but at least the choice of poems was guided by the fundamental realization that one of the deep forms of wealth in South Africa is its multiplicity of languages. This possibility had been almost entirely ignored in previous anthologies, internalising the policy and effects of apartheid, and, more surprisingly, ignored or at least not fully exploited in many anthologies put together since then.

I am struck by the small number of writers (with some notable exceptions) who have in any consistent way engaged themselves in translating texts out of South African languages other than their own. This is no doubt a complex question, with issues of power and race and the politics of publishing at its root. Barriers as thick as coiled razor wire have historically obstructed literary exchange across languages in South Africa, and it will no doubt still be a long time before this situation changes in any radical way.

Nevertheless, I hope that readers of this anthology will appreciate the many angles, amongst them cultural and linguistic, from which both the local situation and universal themes are spoken of by poets represented here. With further development of poetry translation in South Africa, this diversity could well be even richer.

In the Heat of Shadows is in a sense a sequel to *The Lava of this Land*, in which I assembled poems published between 1960 and 1996. That anthology, which includes the work of twelve poets who reappear here, was brought out in 1997 by Northwestern University Press in the

United States, then later by David Philip in Cape Town and in a French version by Actes sud in France.

The immediate opportunity to bring out *In the Heat of Shadows* presented itself in the wake of the Festival international de poètes en Val de Marne (an administrative region just outside Paris), held between 24th May and 2nd June 2013. I was told by the organizers of the festival, Francis Combes and Nelly George-Picot, that one of those hives of poetic activity which dot the French landscape, the Maison de la poèsie Rhône-Alpes, impressed by the reading of South African poets in Grenoble, wanted to bring out an anthology of South African poetry in French translation. I offered to edit this, adding a number of further poets to the fourteen originally invited to the festival, who were: Gabeba Baderoon, Robert Berold, Vonani Bila, Finuala Dowling, Keorapetse Kgositsile, Rustum Kozain, Joan Metelerkamp, Karen Press, Mongane Wally Serote, Ari Sitas, Bulelani Zantsi, Ingrid de Kok and Ronelda Kamfer (neither of them able to attend), and myself. The anthology, *Pas de blessure, pas d'histoire*, came out in November 2013.

The Festival international des poètes en Val de Marne, planned on a bi-annual basis, happened in 2013 to be the prelude to a whole season of South African culture in France, just as there had been a season of French culture in South Africa in 2012. During one of the readings at the festival, I met both Laurent Clavel of the Institut français, French curator of the South African Season, his deputy Bénédicte Alliot, and also Monica Newton, CEO of the National Arts Council of South Africa. Together, and on the spur of the moment, we raised the possibility of bringing out an English version of the anthology. With a minimum of difficulty this has now been concretized, thanks largely to funding from the National Arts Council, with the help of Maggie Reddy and Rosie Katz. Thus the anthologies in French and English not only exist in their own right, but are a legacy of the richly significant Seasons, as well as partially being an offspring of the Festival international de poètes en Val de Marne, a festival as rich and enjoyable as it was fertile ground for exchange between poets of many countries around the world.

20

My warmest thanks, then, to Francis Combes and Nelly George-Picot as well as Anne Segal of the Festival international de poètes en Val de Marne; to those members of the Val-de-Marne region, under its elected president Christian Favier, who generously co-hosted the festival; to Laurent Clavel and Bénédicte Alliot of the Institut français; to Monica Newton, as well as Maggie Reddy and Rosie Katz of the National Arts Council of South Africa. Equally warm thanks to Brigitte Daïan, Pierre Vieuguet, Carole Durand and the entire team of the Maison de la poèsie Rhône-Alpes who gave me a free hand in constituting the French anthology which was made in tandem with this one. Jacques Alvarez-Pereyre, associated with the Maison de la poésie Rhône-Alpes, long active in disseminating and writing about South African poetry here in France, must also be acknowledged for his encouragement of this project.

I must also mention those essential actors in this book whose presence should constantly be borne in mind, especially since their job here is not to affirm their own presence but rather to ally their voices with those of the poets. These are the translators, who practice an art which is nothing less than an act of writing itself: Mike Dickman, Richard Jurgens, Siphiwe ka Ngwenya, Sindiwe Magona, Ike Muila and JC (Koos) Oosthuysen. Thanks, too, to Liz Gowans for her meticulous work on the proofs. I should also say how glad I am that Maja Maljevic was prepared to collaborate on this anthology, making available to us a wonderful painting from her "Nirox Diaries" series for the cover of the book.

More than anyone else, thanks to Robert Berold, most faithful, generous and perceptive of friends and poetic comrade-in-arms; thanks for encouragement, sharp nudges, and for taking the necessary steps, as the publisher of Deep South, to actually get this book into print.

DENIS HIRSON

ANTJIE KROG

Country of grief and grace (extracts)

(a)

between you and me
how desperately
how it aches
how desperately it aches between you and me

so much hurt for truth
so much destruction
so little left for survival

where do we go from here

your voice slung
in anger
over the solid cold length of our past

how long does it take
for a voice
to reach another

in this country held bleeding between us

(b)

in the beginning is seeing
seeing for ages

filling the head with ash
no air
no tendril
now to seeing speaking is added
and the eye plunges into the wounds of anger
seizing the surge of language by its soft bare skull
hear oh hear
the voices all the voices
all baptised in syllables of blood and belonging
this country belongs to the voices who live in it
it lies at last at the foot
of the stories of saffron and amber
angel hair and barbs,
dew and hay and hurt

(d)

because of you
this country no longer lies
between us but within

it breathes becalmed
after being wounded
in its wondrous throat

in the cradle of my skull
it sings   it ignites
my tongue   my inner ear   the cavity of heart
shudders towards the outline
new in soft intimate clicks and gutturals

OF MY SOUL THE RETINA LEARNS TO EXPAND
DAILY BECAUSE BY A THOUSAND STORIES

I WAS SCORCHED

A NEW SKIN

I am changed for ever   I want to say
forgive me
forgive me
forgive me

you whom I have wronged, please
take me

with you

    (f)

what does one do with the old
which already robustly stinks of the new
the old virus slyly manning the freshly installed valves
how does one recognise the old
     with its racism and slime
its unchanging possessive pronoun
what is the past tense of the word hate
what is the symptom of brutalised blood
of pain that did not want to become language
     could not become language

what does one do with the old
how do you become yourself among others
how do you become whole
how do you get released into understanding
how do you make good
how do you cut clean

how close can the tongue teeter to tenderness
or the cheek to forgiveness
a moment
a line which says: from this point onwards
    it is going to sound differently
because all our words lie next to one another on the table
    now
shivering in the colour of human
we know each other well
each other's scalp and smell   each other's blood
we know the deepest sound of each other's kidneys in the night
we are slowly each other
anew
new
and here it starts

poet becoming

to awake one morning into sound
with the antennae of vowel and consonant and diphthong
to calibrate with delicate care the subtlest
movement of light and loss in sound

to find yourself suddenly kneeling at the audible
palpable outline of a word – searching
for that precise moment in which
a poetic line lights up in sound

when the meaning of a word yields, slips
and then surrenders into tone – from then on

the blood yearns for that infinite pitch of a word
because: the only truth stands skinned in sound

the poet writes poetry with her tongue
yes, she breathes deeply with her ear

arrival

the abundance of her tiny skull we do not
grasp. under her hair, one by one
small leaves fold to bone so that her
little face like a lamp overflows with

light and we can see the rose syllables
of her hands or the rustle of a smile
as it glides up into her newborn eyes
prevailing upon them to stay in this

valley of breath. her feet ladling a glow
as we lay her down in milk and fold
her tight. from so many selves

she's had to salvage her own deepest self
before her arrival as our
tiniest bullet of beloved light

morning tea

while she makes tea something strangely
familiar flows down her inner thigh. like ink.
after many years she bleeds again.

she stands overcome – as if a whole orchard
had blossomed up in her throat, as if an old-fashioned
happiness were leaking into her body she feels she's

opening shutters to reveal apples,
shades that haze with birds and cicadas
and sweltering distances – as if a

child's laughter had overflowed in a bath
turning her cheeks vulnerable – intimately
blushed through with daily closeness

as if her abdomen had swelled young and
strong again around her once most beautiful self;
her neck gives in to so much light

she carries the tea out onto the stoep
the sky slakes soft for this time of the
morning; the city glistens like a brimming dam

he comes to sit next to her. peacefully he
stirs his tea. in this way they sit
so far left behind in loss and for their age

so carefully rare in closeness

how do you say this

I truly don't know how to say this
your seasoned neatly clipped beard is perhaps
too here, too close for language, too grey with grit

I really don't know how to write your ageing body
without using words like 'loss' or 'fatal'. I don't know.
I don't know why the word 'wrinkle' sounds so banal
I simply do not know how ageing should sound in language

in the meantime the irises of your infamous blue eyes
have over the years buckled under green
more stuttering now but two enduring sincere

shadows that have loved me a whole life long
my forefinger traces your eyebrows
from where grey hair crackles like lightning
face that I love; face of erosion

if I pull you towards me your hair is thin and light
your scalp surprises me with its own texture
the grooves cutting down from your ears

the mouth that could scathe so brilliantly still
moves fragrantly against my temples but mild now
– as bread   your hands allow my breasts to sink into
your palms like glasses of dark wine I think I'm

trying to say that I find the thickening of your
abdomen attractive, that an erection against a
slight curve wets the mouth god I think

I'm trying to say that I can surrender to
your thighs for the very first time because of
their soaked-ness, that I prefer the soft
looseness of your buttocks to the young

aggressive passion of our youth you no longer
use sex for yourself but for me you no longer
want to breed children from me but calmly reveal

yourself into the luxury of experience I
stretch myself deeper quieter
as if we come to be much more complete.
at times it seems easier to rage

against the dying of the light
than to eke out
the vocabulary of old age

sonnet of the hot flushes

something staples your marrow somewhere
you feel a newly floated fire spreading angst from
a kernel and how your veins run with fire how
your flesh flames your heart keeps her fireproof
balance your bones roast besides themselves your
face singes your cheeks simmer in dismay and
time and again you break out in sizzling encasings
of sweat you smell your skin sparking off a blaze

but one day you shift in your chair – and
feel this great crucible destroying your

last sap   God knows, this is enough:
burning like a warrior you rise – a figurehead of
fire – you grab this death like a runt and plough its nose
right through your fleeced and drybaked cunt

Winter

wednesday 18 june
I cannot look at you
today, not today. with eyes averted
from your stony perfection
I do my daily chores.

over my terrified
body my hand moves up to
my breast again hoping
that the lump of clay will not be there
that the hand misconstrued

the mountain stands
stripped clean and burnt through. I live by the
breath of this mountain alone.
I have no other competence. on
the windward side fringes of light sing, on
the lee side there is nought

not even a single
line that knows of me. mortality
sticks to my lip like sweat.
I want to know/not to know/to know
everything/know nothing

thursday 19 june
invisible mountain this morning
in this mist – a lump of grief against
which everything flounders.
softly your thoughts try to probe around
it   gently you sense the
embedded stone, the numbness of it

the immobility,
you don't have the courage to fathom
the full extent, you just
await the result. from the waist up you
blindly suppose yourself
secretly whole, you try to defuse

your body's insurgence
against your body. let the stone lump
grow cold in the fog, let
the pine trees tilt like umbrellas in
a cortège, let my thoughts
steam to ripeness in sorrow. but I,

I am occupied this
morning: softly I coax my breasts to
unwind in foam, let them
freely drowse in tranquil fragrance
rinse them in honey
to luminous shape and there where the

mammogram reveals its
blackest clot, I lather in light
and
light-
limbed

bliss
so

blindingly that the black membrane
feels
itself blessed, diluting its
toxic polyps,
dissolving them to effluence. see
the rust bleeding away like beestings.
whole like a whiplash

I want to live on this earth.
                    (late night)
fuck-all. I feel fuck-all
for the life hereafter – it's *now* that
I want to live, *here*

is what I want

sunday 22 june
nothing arrives. my throat
constricts. a resigned grief burns up in
my chest, smoking. my heart
whimpers on her hinges. I want to
touch something, hold something,
revive the wholeness that once was mine.

I want to return with
my previous body. I am not
I, without my body
only through my body can I in-
habit this earth. my soul
is my body entire. my body

embodies
do not turn against me, oh do not
ever leave me. do not
cave in around me, do not plummet
away from me, do not
die off on me, step
into the breach for me –
my only mandate to
engage the earth

monday 23 june
I no longer dwell
on the word 'malignant', it's
the word 'benign'
that makes my skin slip like a gorgeous
silk scarf round my body.
I breathe freely. the air has quickened.
I drink my morning tea. my
eyes consume the mountain in stately
gait
(though something, what I
do not know, has surfaced quietly –
a deadly silence
encrusts the windows –
has mortality come on
board? is the body beginning to take its leave?)

friday 27 june
the last rains of winter fall
faster than the yearning of winter trees
with lymphatic systems
against the wintry light. benign
benign – it's as if

I am young again in
my upper arms, suddenly, and smooth
at the back of my head.
my body glows complete, my elbows
hang free with my senses
extended over my skin.
I want to
ascend
in this body
roaring its immaculate radiance

Translated from the Afrikaans by Antjie Krog.

ROBERT BEROLD

To my room

When I moved here you were much darker,
so I put in windows and the aerial bookshelf
that runs around above head height. Now
I sleep with a weight of books above me.
I want to cover them, like birds, to keep them quiet.

I've slept three thousand nights in your arms.
You have absorbed my snoring and my dreams.
Your walls have seen dogs, spiders, frogs, snakes too,
and once a porcupine ambled through.

The trees are coming into leaf today.
I tell you this slowly because you've never been outside.

The water running

the water running in the gullies
the hoopoe bobbing, flying off abruptly

the sky full of leftover rain
nokwakwa weeding bent straight at the waist

the grass bright green after the fire
the hoopoe in the grass a nervous king

the bakkie loaded up for town
the pipes and ditches swollen with water

the tierhout burnt
the yellowwood burnt

the burnt veld
the water running

All the days

Still autumn day, horizon on all sides,
the old dog snoring in the sun. Butter-yellow
sunlight illuminates a honeysuckle shrub
in which a furtive shrike half-scuttles.

                         The bell rings
it's Zanemvula, he wants something to eat, he's sick
and thin, not functioning in his fear-filled world.
Blue card, he says, he wants his unemployment card.
I say: There are no more blue cards, they use computers now.
I give him bread with Black Cat peanut butter, and two oranges.

                Zwelenzima's digging out the telephone poles,
they've had their day, the signal goes by microwave now
because of all the theft of copper wire. The poles
look strange lying horizontal by the road, their white
ceramic insulators like tumours.

I've just caught up
several months of debt, and I'm driving to town,
with spring water and vegetables, in my one-eyed bakkie –
its headlamp fell out on the shaky road the other night.
It will be repaired on Monday when the part arrives from PE.

In August
I'm going to China, to live among a thousand million people.
Who will take care of Mindy? Who will take care of my cat?
Who will take care of all the days that pass through here?

The phone rings,
it's a wrong number, a text message converted electronically
into a male computer voice which says:
"I'm sending this from my mom's phone.
I miss you very very much. Maria.
I'm sending this from my mom's phone.
I miss you very very much. Maria."

I think of Maria
I think of the wind carrying silence and autumn light.

The rock thrushes

The rock thrushes have two sounds, an aggressive warning
of loud clicks, and a whistling song. The song, sung by the
male, has fixed notes and rhythms, then he improvises at
the end. I whistle the rock thrush song to them and they
check me out with their 270-degree vision. They sing every
day, even in the rain.

I love their plumpness and their boldness. Whenever they can, they come into the house, especially the female. Not fazed by my moving around, she hops two-legged along the wooden beam to get a better look at me. And then she flies out confidently, through the open door.

This is the third generation of rock thrushes since I've been here. The first male was a serious musician, with complex improvisations. The second hardly whistled at all. This one is more of a pop singer, not straying from the theme tune, and louder than the others.

My cat got some of the second generation, but these ones are sharp. The male is a brighter colour than the previous ones, his chest a redder rust, his slate blue head more blue. The female dives down to steal a catfood pellet from the bowl.

Letter to Mary

I tried to get to see your grandchildren. I phoned the only shop at Sepanaphudi. A manual operator put me through. I asked him if he knew the Theleles. Yes, he said, they're all here, who do you want to speak to?

I phoned the next day, spoke to one of them. Didn't get his name but he knew mine. Mr Robert? – Come and see us quickly. Bring clothes, girls' clothes, and food. We are all without job. Can you come tomorrow? Put off by his desperation, I didn't go.

I'll still come one of these days and visit your grave. Long
ago you carried me from the noise into the sunlight. How
much I've tried to pay my debt to you. Only to find that
debts of guilt are endless. And debts of love? There are
no debts of love.

Visit to my mother

The pink and red impatiens in her garden
look artificial. And the lawn too green. But all
of Rosebank and its malls look artificial now.
I feel stranded among her fish forks and knives.
The family photos have congealed inside their frames.

"Do you believe in evolution?" she asks. "That's a fact,"
I say, "it's not a matter of belief." She doesn't like the fact
that humans started off in Africa. "What about
the different races? And the different cultures? How
can they work these things out from a pile of old skulls?"

"The Sunday Times has a black editor, hasn't it?"
"Yes," I say. "That's why it's full of sex" she says.
"It's always been," I say, "and anyway
those stories come from British newspapers."
"It's even more these days," she says,

"that's all they're interested in – sex and thieving."
Her racism is savage as ever.
I've come to see her because she's been ill.

In intensive care. She could have died.
"They all pinch" she says.

"Last month they pinched a car
from the parking garage." Pinch – that's the word
she uses. She seems quite healthy now
except she has a pinched nerve in her spine,
she has to use a wheelchair or a walking frame.

"Do you believe in reincarnation?" she asks.
She's 86. "I believe in everything," I say.
"Well I don't," she says. "I've been so weary recently,
so old, so tired. I do believe in God, though.
I don't know why, because I'm cynical. Do you?"

"Believe in God? Sure, but I prefer the Dao.
Less anthropomorphic." "Less what?" The TV is on
much too loud. "I have no talent," she says, "I've never had a talent."
"You've always been bright. And you're still alert," I say,
"surely you have some redeeming qualities?"

"A sense of humour," she says, "it's helped me stay around
this long. And I like having happy people round me."
Maki, her live-in nurse, seems happy (and she doesn't pinch).
My mother's hair is getting thin. "God," I think, "I'm almost 60,
my hair is white too, and most of it is gone." I think:

"59 years ago I was in this woman's womb."
Her soup spoon clatters in her plate.
"Well I'll be gone soon, to the next world,
and none of you will miss me". My youngest
brother Grant arrives, he's visiting her as well.

"Why did you go into psychotherapy?" he asks me.
We'd started talking about this yesterday
when he fetched me from the airport. My mother answers
"Therapy is when you pay a lot of money to someone
to tell you that you had bad parents."

"Things were a mess for me," I tell him. "My life just
wasn't working." "But couldn't you work out your problems
and then leave them behind?" "Yes" my mother says, "we all
had to get on with it." "Maybe for you" I say to him, "but for me
the story had to be untangled first. It took a lot of time."

Next day she says "You're right, I was
a bad mother. I was too anxious. I apologise."
"That's OK," I say. "I accept your apology."
"I go down on my bended knees," she says.
"Don't ruin it with sarcasm," I reply.

A meeting with her accountants. Her finances are healthy.
Her car needs a service. She can't drive anymore but
it's there for her three sons when we visit her in Joburg.
"You can't stop worrying about your chirrun," she says.
That's the way she says it. Chirrun. I kiss her on the head goodbye.

angel

just when you don't know anymore
an angel arises
maybe an angel of paradise
as you are driving up Claim Street
and turn the corner into total confusion

maybe an angel of sadness
or an angel of summer who lives beside you
who sings beside you with the noise of bees

just when you don't know anymore
when you really don't know
an angel arises

KAREN PRESS

Glass cabinet: the watch

It's always a watch, in the end,
as if you'll need help counting the hours you have left
now that no one records your coming and going.

But this one was different.
A watch for a woman who'd spent sixty years
catching each watch as it was born, wiping it clean of its maker's
    smudges,
swaddling it in velvet and foam, sending it into the world
and taking it back for nursing and consolation each time it collapsed
under the strain of time's greedy demands.

A watch made of diamonds and mother of pearl,
best work of the master craftsman, hers to keep.
One diamond for every hour of the working day,
the white hours and the yellow hours.

The same day over and over,
sparkling and fading as the sun moved across its face.

Blessed are the ones who work with love
and blessed are those who make things with their hands and
    their souls.

Blessed are they who go out every day to switch on the
    world's machines
and leave the print of their eyes on all tools and materials.

Blessed are they who repeat actions with increasing seriousness
    and stillness,
and blessed are the ones who look up dreamily from their work
    benches and smile, seeing the other heads bent around them.

Blessed are the children who want to mould mud into shapes they
    can name.
Blessed are the lovers who leave each other every day to give
    themselves to the world.

Blessed is the watchmaker who clasps time in his fingers
and blessed is the old lady who has polished it every day and takes it
    home with her at last.

Praise poem: I saw you coming towards me (extract)

Once you came towards us bravely as rushing river water.
You flowed thunderously and sweetly towards us with your
    understanding.

Now you trickle through that same river bed
like the thinnest trail of spittle left by a sick man,
your roar clatters like pebbles thrown by boys into dry gutters.

Your breath sets fire to the frail crops.
Your feet stamp the floor of the house until it breaks open.

You whose blood is as dark as the blood of a lion
when it has been poisoned by honey from the hives of a nation,
eaten and spilled wide across the floors of so many houses –

on your way home you renounce the peacock's feathers,
    mocking them
and take for yourself the leopard's pelt as if it was your own.
See there where the peacock comes to meet you at your front door,
he will walk ahead of you to sing your coming,
you wear him alive and whole
and the leopard's corpse rots in the hearth, in your mother's hearth
    it rots.

Man who, when you come among us
makes our bodies seem to grow fat
and our clothes shine in your hot shadow,
but when you leave we see we are as thin as worn shafts
and our shirts have shrivelled to muddy rags.

Your legs had the strength of tree trunks when you strode towards us
but now they are shrivelled, you are a man walking on old canes
    chewed by rats.

Man of three legs standing astride our land like the feast pot
you make us believe we can kill hunger while you rise over us
but you eat your food yourself, your shadow fattens
while we watch with wide mouths.

You landlord of the dreams of people,
hunter of our hopes who captures them
like an old bear that can no longer eat,
eagle with the ragged beak of a vulture –
beware the winter hour when your wings fail you,
beware the hungry boys with stones waiting
in the street where you will land, where you will wander whimpering
among the piles of refuse left by your armies.

I saw you coming towards me
from far away.

From far away
I recognised you.

Do you love yourself like this

Do you love yourself like this,
former warrior
bursting with luxury
in your narrow parliamentary seat?
Does your body enjoy being this big?

Did you imagine
it would turn out like this?
As you walk into court
between your lawyer and your wife
do you feel proud
of your arms-deal-payola 4x4?
Are you ready to die
to defend it
from being repossessed?

I hope so.
I hope this all has meaning for you,
this ugly life you've chosen
after so much struggle.

I want all people to be happy,
even you.

I hope you feel proud of yourself,
I do.
(Someone has to.)
You were so beautiful once.

*

You once had to try and survive
death by wet bag torture
and the knees of a man
in your kidneys, pressing harder, harder..

Does your car compensate for that?
Is that what makes you feel you deserve
the bespoke suit and shirt and tie
stretched tight around your swollen neck?

I worry that you'll think this question
snide or cynical. It isn't – I want to know
if that's the reasoning that works for your integrity.

Some people say
what you're doing now
simply confirms what your politics were
all along.

I'm not one of them –
I think, Stalinism and the sneering shadow flitting across your eyes
notwithstanding, that you had something to fight for,
something greater than clothes and a car,
more lithe, more radiant inside its own skin.
You were so beautiful then.

Pasternak's shadow

The chapter recounts how Stalin phoned Pasternak
to ask who Mandelstam was, if he was a 'master' –
and explains what Pasternak surely knew at once,
that Stalin was asking whether and what he would lose
if he followed his first instinct: to kill the poet.
Yes, Pasternak told him, Mandelstam is a master,
and saved the poet's life
for the endlessness of an exile
and the whisper of a prison death.

What made Stalin feel threatened
by this small man's unwritten poem?
the chapter goes on to ask and struggles to answer,
but I've stayed behind
in the room where Pasternak looks at the telephone,
I can see how his hand is shaking
as he breathes in what he's just done.

Of course Mandelstam is a master
and if he, Pasternak, with one clear syllable uttered in a daze
has saved the poet's life for the time it takes
a small boy to swoop past him on his toboggan,
his red face brighter than the sun of this unending winter,
he can live with himself another day
inside Stalin's cold protective shadow.

But the question that rises up
like the shadow of that shadow
will not leave him now,
it clings to his soul like a forest leech:
if it had been another poet,
if it had been the man three streets away

who shows him his dull rhymes about birches and soldiers
or the woman whose love poems
have been clogging his letter box for years,
if it had been the professor who writes stale odes
in praise of nothing living,
would he have called each one 'master'
for the sake of their lives?

Would he stand up inside the mask of his freedom
and burn his own fine-tuned tongue
to keep one of them warm?
He wants to tear the telephone loose from its wall
so that there can be no more –
but he dare not – what if Stalin has Akhmatova's name
scrawled on a pad in front of him,
with a question mark?

Walking songs for Africans abroad

A travelling game

There's a game we play when we travel abroad.
Looking up from a drink in a bar, a museum queue, a souvenir counter
we ask, where are the Africans?

We ask, where are the Africans?
And we answer each other in different ways
depending on the mood we're in.
It's a way to pass through the hours of estrangement,
a way to walk through the galleries of strange looks from strangers.

The game ends when one of us says,
that's a non-question.

Or when we realise there are non-African friends among us
looking hurt, or starting to apologise for something.
We change the subject then. It's seldom worth the effort
of trying to explain this isn't about them.

One of us alone may ask the question silently
stepping out into the morning of a foreign city,
like a ghost setting out to haunt an unfamiliar house.
It's a way of comforting ourselves, recalling that there must be
other ghosts like us, and that we all haunt houses where we've never
    lived.

At Lago di Garda they have other problems

Lago di Garda is a beautiful place, laced with settings for Goethe's
    dreams of the south.
Walking along the narrow road between Sompriezzo and Pieve
you understand at last the things in your childhood anthologies:
cowbells, hazelnut trees, Jews hidden in caves and barns, bramble berries.

Around the lake itself cypresses preen, lemon groves pretend an ancient
    elegance
and the *gelati* are pistachio, vanilla, cherry and lime just as they should
    be.
I looked around unrestfully, not knowing why.
The light was chiffon everywhere, a kind of silence
filtering the chatter of the promenade away from anything true.

I thought I saw a dark shape walking up a side street
and my skin changed as if someone familiar had touched me.

51

But it was gone, or never there; only the cool palazzo walls stared past me.
I knew I must be the only person in this whole town who could even
   imagine
what my real world is like, so much light and earth, so much sleeping and
   growing.

But later I watched the tired owner of the *gelateria* locking his doors
and realised he'd probably been trying to speak German all day to
   Bavarian tourists.
Nobody really cares what anyone else's world is like, unless they're writing
   a PhD.
It's not a crime against humanity.

Thesaurus entries for "Africans abroad"

in transit
transitory
transitional
transient

The sociological fraud

If you ask the wrong question, you get the wrong answer.
An African taught me that.

I ask them anyway, when I get lonely.
The answers astonish each time, like onions.

For example:
Why is the first human you see at any airport
a black man handling luggage?

Why do American novelists still divide their characters
into "characters" and "black characters"?

Why are there no African skinheads or *au pairs*?

At conferences we learn so much

To stand inside your theories, unuttered,
produces a dizziness. Caught between the lushness of my world
and its absence here. Do you think your ruling class's surplus capital
came from a hole in the ground in Greenland?

Talking and talking you talk, my dedicated friends,
and all that you know teeters on a point of blindness
your toes fail to sense, clutching the soles of your feet,
thinking they are the whole earth's curve supporting you.

Local rabbits in smart jeans, you're thermally well-protected and
    anxious for change,
just checking the time on your perfect watches.
Do you ever look at your backs in the mirror?
From my country we see them all the time,
the raw edges, the sand trickling out of the seams, the drought-
    stricken heels.
Millions of tiny seamstresses still working on you.

You welcome us, we are your cautionary tales, your myths, your
    keynote speakers,
the parts of you that walked across the mined desert to get here.
You wish you could have a miracle like ours,
a sort of atom bomb of festivity to clear the past out of the way.

The puzzled looks on our faces you take for a problem of language,
and devote yourselves to whispering translations of the speeches in our
  ears.
You're right, in a sense; we don't have a language for saying
where do your questions come from?

Hanging around in corners like one of Jane Austen's minor girls,
I'm trying to tuck my continent in behind me
so no-one trips on it. But it's so damned big.
I should never have tried to bring it with me.

"Wear ethnic dress," they ask all delegates.
As if history were a diorama in a department store window
and not the bright patterns of blood on all our bedroom floors.
Their ethnic dress is black leather with a touch of something striped.
Nepalese, Guatemalan.
Very cool.

Born travellers

We're born travellers. We compose walking songs, songs of building
the boss's roads, songs of the long train journey to the mines, songs
of our lovers abandoning us for city women, songs of living in hostels
without our children, of standing at passport offices, of being in
exile, of tracking a cow or a lion or a USAID management studies
programme. We invented a piano the size of our hearts to play as we
walk.

We've been travelling forever. There's a map that shows how Africans
spread across the world to populate it; the cartographers called it
"Africans: the first colonisers". Some of us have objected to being
called that. We're more comfortable with the modest role of loving
our birthplace and wanting it back. But we keep on travelling, in the

holds of ships and down mine shafts, with crates of goods to sell and dossiers of crimes to recount. We have so much left to give, so many blood diamonds and bleached bones, so many muted languages and ecstatic dances. Over and over again we re-populate the world with our evolving pain and curiosity, replenishing each present moment with the DNA of history.

"At the round earth's imagined corners"

After another one of those trips
someone sees his colleague at the airport queuing for the pay phone
and says, "E T phone home ..."
and she says "This *is* home, aren't we the world's brothers and sisters?"
and he says, "Tell that to the passport officers"
and they laugh, and inside they each feel a little sick,
and on the plane each one wakes at some point during the flight
to jot down a few words in a diary, notes for a song or a poem.

A cow and a goose

A cow and a goose came to my door one day.

"We don't want to die," they said with one voice.

There are so many different ways to respond to two strange animals
who come to your door and say something like that.
For example, "Why not?" and "We all have to die."
or, "What do you expect me to do about that?"
or, "Why are you here?"
but especially, "Where did you learn to speak English?"

I felt too confused to say anything at all.
To my shame I put out a saucer of milk
and went back to my novel.

The next day they came back.
"I'm sorry," I said this time. "The milk was stupid."
Then I was stuck.

They wandered around my garden for a bit,
to give me time to come up with something more useful.
When they got back to where I was standing they said again,
slightly more slowly, "We really don't want to die."

"Nor do I," I said.
It was the only true thing that came to mind.

Vonani Bila

In the name of Amandla

In the name of Amandla
Tell me what has changed in this village
There's no food in the kitchen
Bare children with chapped lips can't go to school
Another hungry child knocked down by a rich man's car
The child is gone, the rich man contributed a cheap coffin
Everyone thought he would rot in prison
It's winter, the school has no desks, textbooks & windows
Our leaders send their children to private schools
Ask them

In the name of Amandla
Tell me what has changed in this village
The tap is dry
Coughs hot air
The pump is off
Granny has no cash to buy diesel
She walks distances to draw dirty water
In the still pool
In the poisoned dam
Where people share water with animals
Granny washes in a cracked red plastic basin
She buys water and pushes a wheelbarrow
She is old, 70!
Her hut collapsed during the days of the flood
She survived, because she was busy collecting wood in the bush
She waited for her pension at 65 years of age
She stands in a queue, shoving and shuffling
Someone of her age collapses in the smothering sun

She closes her eyes, sniffs snuff
She sneezes, tears run down her cheeks
She gets her pension, it's a cheque

In the name of Amandla
Tell me what has changed in this village
Magogo takes a taxi to town
Young ones don't want to sit next to her
They say she smells of urine
She buys a tin of paraffin, a blanket and chicken
She buys a bag of mealiemeal on account
Her daughters, now mothers, want their share
Government gives R110 per child
Granny pays the burial society every month
She does not want to be buried in a blanket
People won't come to the funeral if a cow is not slaughtered
She talks alone, predicts death anytime from now
She is called a 'cheque' by her own daughters
Their husbands are unemployed
They weave & sell baskets, smoke BB & drink mqombhothi
They wait to reach 65 to caress coins
Magogo washes in a cracked red plastic basin
She wants to take a shower before she dies
She calls Mandela 'Mondela'
She only votes for the ANC
Why?

In the name of Amandla
Tell me what has changed in this village
We are in trouble
Our electricity is weak
Switch off everything else when you use a stove
It stops when it rains
It flies away with the wind

Come winter – the municipality will cut it off
Poor black man in arrears
Back to *mbhawula* and *malahla*
Magogo is cold
She sleeps by the fire
Burning her feet
The brazier emits gas
She will cough blood clots
Health worker at the clinic will give her panados

In the holy name of Amandla
Tell me what has changed in this village
Our RDP house leaks when it rains
We can't fit, it's a toilet
We hear & see them making love
In a room divided by a curtain
There can't be any secrets
We sleep in the kitchen
Wake up like elephants early in the morning
Verwoerd, my enemy, built much bigger houses
Trevor Manuel can't stop buying submarines, corvettes and jetfighters
Our taxes can do something better
War is coming we are told.

Ancestral Wealth

For my father Risimati Daniel Bila: 1931-1989

I

Under these tall thorn umbrella trees
My ancestors dwell
Jonas is buried in a woven grass kenya
When Dayimani woke up dead at 10 am
He was buried in the afternoon, the same day
His body covered with white linen and a thin blanket
My ancestors dwell here
Seated, facing home in the east
Facing Bileni, far away in Mozambique
A broken mattress and xihlungwani *heaped on the grave*
Cracked enamel plates and mugs heaped on the grave

II

Papa, when you finally got admitted at Giyani Block
We thought the learned doctors who can see what's hidden in blood
    and water
Would remove these needles
And pins and spears in your veins and wearied bones
But their bewitched green-red flashing machines in theatre confirmed you
    healthy
And when you got into the late night train ride to Garankuwa Hospital
Far away in Pretoria, on that ultra-distance bumpy ride
We thought the learned doctors would have removed this excruciating pain
In your chest and packing-up bones
But doctors in white gowns saw no fault in your stuttering engine

They sent you home
You got into that long bumpy train ride uncured
They asked you to come with your wife on 4th December 1989
For possible heart surgery
And the next day you came back home
Sat with your family around the fire
That night you didn't cough blood clots, nor groan
That night you didn't vomit
Nor was your body a river of sweat
Your face was sun-beaming
Blue eyes were shining
We ate chicken stew and pap
Drank Rooibos tea with buttered bread
That night owls and the wind didn't howl in trees
The mountain snake and dzelehani didn't cry
Dogs and cats didn't wail nor mew
That night I slept like a baby

Under these tall thorn umbrella trees
My ancestors rise and hold hands
They sing in unison
Dance in rhythmic step
Around the fire

III

Wednesday 13 September 1989, 1 am:
You asked mother to extinguish the paraffin lamp
Burning on the red polished cement floor
The time to switch off your tormented heart beat had beckoned
That day you requested mhani N'wa-Noel
Your concubine from Mbhokota
To sleep in the grass-thatched rondavel with your girl children

Because the last night of intimacy
And pain belonged to your wife Fokisa N'wa-Mahatlani
Your black beauty of twenty six years
Yena wa ka mkhamu wa nsuku na ngwavila (She whose body glitters with
  gold and gems)
Mbati ya ku fuma (The door to wealth)

Your last night belonged to your wife
Who birthed you seven healthy children
Children born between 1964 and 1980
The last night to outline your will –
Because you knew *n'wana wa munhu u le kusuhani*
The last night to outline how your homestead should be run
So that you don't return home wearing shorts
And run riot
In case your house was turned into a playground
Emachihweni, emathumbhanini
You sat on your three quarter bed
Wearing that brown striped t-shirt from Pep stores
Eyes fixed on the old leaking zinc roof
Then you paged through the Old Mutual policy document
And you said:
Mhana Oom (he called me Oom)
The roof is old
I have bought the bricks
But they'll not be enough to build a decent house
When they give you my little pension fund
Build a house:
A room for Oom, a room for Simon, another room for Makhanani and Julia
If God had given me seven more years to live
Oom and Simon would be working
They would take care of Makhanani and Julia
Then the burning paraffin lamp was extinguished:
Each sleeping in their separate three quarter beds

Suddenly a heavy hand whipped mother's shoulder
It was her grandmother N'wa-Xakhombo
Whose voice shrieked:
Pfuka wena N'wa-Mafelalomo (Wake up, you who die in far distant places)
A wu swi voni leswaku wa weriwa? (Don't you see the roof is falling,
  collapsing upon you?)
All she heard was one groan
Hhmmm, hmmmm!
And Papa, when she came to your three quarter bed
Daniel Risimati Bila the son of Dayimani and N'wa-Zulu
Had packed for good
Papa, your room was filled with cold air
Misty cloudy smog covered the room at 1am
Mama says you didn't hit or kick the walls violently
As you wrestled with the monster
Kwalaho ndzi n'wi longa (Then I laid out his body)
Ndzi koka minkumba ndzi zola milenge (I removed blankets and
  elevated his legs)
Ndzi lola mavoko ya longoloka na yena (I elevated his hands and arms
  along his body)
Ndzi vuyetela mahlo (I gently closed his eyes with a simple touch)
Ndzi n'wi sula xikandza (I wiped down his face)
A hlambile a nga se etlela (He had bathed before bedtime)
Mapfalo ya mina a ma file (I was but remorseless)
Ivi ndzi khomelela mubedwa (Then I held the bed so firm)
Ndzi ku kumbe u ta pfuka (Thinking that he would wake up)
She searched for Rattex in the wardrobe
If she had found it
She would have crushed it
Swallowed it to burn her liver and heart
And join you in the other world
How would she raise her children
With cents from selling bananas and tomatoes
At the Elim market?

63

Under these tall thorn umbrella trees
My ancestors rise and hold hands
They sing in unison
Dance in rhythmic step
Around the fire

IV

"My time to go has arrived," you told mother several times
The ZCC prophets Markos Mukhuva and vho-Ramantshwane
Had tearfully told you the same at Magangeni church:
Your life's ticket is over
They told you a few months before your departure
To the land yonder
They told you to stop chasing after the skirts
Because skirts were a cloth covering a big bottomless pit
And you came home to tell your wife
You were not taking anyone's cows nor calves in the kraal
But helping the wandering women in need
You lived facing the tomb
Facing the red setting sun
Knowing your living days
Were vanishing fast like paraffin paper fire
You lived facing the tomb
Knowing you couldn't afford skipping monthly subscriptions
To Saffas the undertaker in Louis Trichardt
Because the ancestors *emaxubini* were calling you
You lived facing the tomb
That's why you cleared the bushy shrubs
Making the road with a pick and shovel
Making the road with a spade and hoe
Because you wanted the hearse
To collect your remains at home with ease

Because you didn't want to be loaded in a wheelbarrow
And driven to be collected at the main road
Watched by birds, monkeys and stray dogs
You lived facing the tomb
Because Papa, something so sharp was piercing you
Needles stinging your veins with deadly venom
Nails biting on your flesh
The sharp spear jabbing your heart
Something so sharp was numbing your veins
Draining your energy from your bowels
You breathed heavily every time you climbed a steep hill
You coughed strenuously, sneezing, lungs rattled
Sometimes you collapsed on the narrow paths
After vomiting blood, groaning, vomiting air
Sometimes you bellowed
Like someone who had eaten fresh poison
But Papa, you carried the burden of a family man
On your shoulders
Working every day of the week
Slowly walking ten kilometres every day
To Elim Hospital
For all these thirty years
Helping doctors carry out post-mortems –
Cutting through skulls, stitching and cleaning the dead so stinking
Burying the dead in black shrouds at ten o'clock every day
Behind the hospital sewerage
Papa, you did everything at Elim Hospital:
Ferrying patients to theatre
Feeding relieved mothers at the maternity wards
Scrubbing the floor in the Eye Department
Papa, you did everything at Elim Hospital
Just a for a paltry R300 salary in 1989
Because you had beaks to feed
And clothe

Under these tall thorn umbrella trees
My ancestors rise like elephants
At the break of dawn
To drink water
From the mountain's fountain

V

Saturday 26th September 1989 we hid you
In this sacred ground where shoes are taken off
It's not a cemetery for commoners
It's not Mazokhele nor Avalon
It's the Bila gardens, within my yard
It's a pity you spent two weeks in those mortuary pans
Ice must have burnt your skin and bones
Silencing the sense of hearing that never dies
Burning the growing beard and hair
When Saffas brought you home at dusk on Friday
In that dark hearse
Candles and a paraffin lamp burnt the whole night
In your lonely bedroom
The funeral parlour had bathed you
Dressed in a white silky shroud
Mother and the elderly women wearing blankets
Slept on the floor around the coffin the whole night
In your two-roomed house
Papa, when you left us
Your three quarter bed was removed from the room
Put outside the house against the tree
I was a small boy of seventeen
Doing standard nine at Lemana High
For days I didn't go to school
Even though *a ka ha ri vusiku*

The elders said *ku fanele ku songiwa masangu*
I listened to *Ta lava hundzeke emisaveni* on Radio Tsonga
To hear your name mentioned on that dreadful programme
7am, your light brown casket covered with a blanket
Was displayed in the courtyard
We walked around it to view you for the last time
People cried, some fell to the ground so hard
It was the first time I saw a dead man
And the fallen man was my father
Who in that fateful night
Told mom that had he known better
That he would die prematurely
He wouldn't have fathered his four last children
Including Oom
So I viewed you for the last time on earth
And I shed no tear because death had long come
I had seen you walk away
Eaten by an illness no doctor could detect
The night before the funeral –
I sat around the big fire
Reverend Chabalala was preaching in the crowded tent
Papa, know that John Zulu your uncle donated a beast for the funeral
It was slaughtered *eka* Mapuve
80 kms away from Elim/Shirley
Papa, know that people spoke so well at your burial
Elias Machume was the Programme Director
Hahani N'wa-Risimati Xisana, in tears,
Informed the mourners about your death
And asked your ancestors Dayimani the son of Jonas
Jonas the son of Makhayingi
Makhayingi wa Mpfumari
Mpfumari wa Xanjhinghu
Xanjhinghu wa Ntshovi
Ntshovi wa Xisilafole xi nga ri na nhonga xi sila hi mandla

To receive you on the other side
Your brother John Bila who had disappeared for more than
  twenty years
Came back home the day you died
He trembled, speaking on behalf of the family
Can't remember what he said, because he said nothing, but cried
Your wife's brother J.S. Mashele also paid tribute to you
Even your colleagues from Elim Hospital came in numbers
They sang hymns melodically
P. Mathavha spoke on behalf of the ZCC
Meriam Shetlele represented the neighbourhood
Thomas Mahlasela read the wreaths
Sivara Rev Maluleke, the short and handsome friend of yours,
Carried your coffin to the grave
The ZCC *mokhukhu* men danced in khakhi and *manyanyatha*
Chonaphi Cawuke, Phineas N'wavungavunga, Shilowa,
Mahanci and Xikhudu the great dancers were there
The yard was full of mourners
Men wearing jackets and women draped in blankets
Even The Lion of Judah, your first wife's brother, was there!
He gave the vote of thanks with his moving coarse voice
Mourners contributed cash –
It was recorded in a book. It was good money.
But some members of my family with long fingers
Never showed all the money to my mother
I was still small Papa. But I've forgiven these thieves
We planted your remains
Filled the grave with blood red soil
It had a hump like a bull
The elderly planted maize, beans, corn and pumpkins
Inviting the rain to come
Because your death was never going to bring famine
And starvation in this house
The elderly placed coins and your preferred drinking mug and plate

68

On the grave
We laid you besides your mother Makhanani N'wa-Zulu
Who died on 16 November 1980
And your father Dayimani who died in June 1964
A white cross marked your name:
Daniel Risimati Bila
Rest in peace

Under these tall thorn umbrella trees
My ancestors rise and hold hands
They sing in unison
Dance in rhythmic step
Around the fire

VI

Papa, you came home to rest forever
Because Giyani Block breeds the pungent death smell
Shallow breathing skeletons crumble in the crowded ward
With no family member to preserve their sanity
The jaws lock, eyes fixed
And the white pupils enlarged in the light so bright

Papa, you came home to rest forever
Because shivering patients with bluish lips
Watch tearfully as the final air bursts from the belly
Of a patient next door, bursting like a detonated bomb
Misty air blackening the ward with coldness

The restless patients with irregular pulse
Watch helplessly as the nurses remove the linen
With that stinking last black stool
Transferring this man who died in the night to another ward –

Next to a living patient in a single room
The living patient is happy he's got a neighbour
But the neighbour is fast asleep, wearing a shroud
The new neighbour is neither hungry nor thirsty
The living starts to hallucinate
Gets lost in nappies
Now he knows the nurses brought him a strange ghost
Who'll gnaw at his dreams

Papa, you came home to rest forever
Because in this hospital, like many hospitals
Just an hour after someone has been confirmed dead by the doctor
The nurses make up the same bed
A new patient sleeps in there comfortably
He doesn't know someone has just died there
He collects the spirit of the dead
In the middle of the night
The new patient rushes to the toilet to pray
Pleading to see his only son from Joburg
And when his son arrives the next morning
And holds his father's cold hand
The old man opens his mouth with difficulty
As if to say, my son take care of my cattle
But no word shoots from the mouth layered with white foam
And again goes another patient
In broad daylight

Papa, you came home to rest forever
Because the groaning and wailing movie never stops in the hospital
Some pale-faced patients urinate in coffee mugs and plates
The very same mugs they use for coffee and tea
Some patients jump from the bed like impalas
Tearing drips and tubes away
They race around the ward wearing the catheters

Bubbling with urine tea
They too scream in hallucination:
Nurse, come and help
They are here with knives
They want to suffocate me
They want to cut my throat

In the intensive care unit, someone is motionless
Trapped in a truncation
His car rolled three times into the donga
His head was almost crushed
Perhaps he's brain dead
But the heart is still beating slowly
The nurses feed him
They change his nappies every hour
His family won't allow the medics to
Switch off the life support machine
Because though he's brain dead
Miracles can still happen
They happened in the days of Jesus Christ
And when his spear suddenly rises
The nurses know the brain dead patient's life ticket is still intact

Some burnt-out nurses simply talk on cellphones
Watching this ongoing groaning and vomiting and shitting drama
But you Papa, you didn't want to die like your mother Makhanani
    N'wa-Zulu
Who spent five months at Shangaan Block without eating
Nor going to the toilet on her own
My grandmother who died alone
Who when her coffin was opened for viewing
Even a brave man like you Papa, cried
Because there was no one to close her mouth

71

Papa, you came home to rest forever
Like Dayimani your father
And Jonas your grandfather
And Makhayingi your great grandfather
You came home to rest forever
After a family meal
In the hands of your wife
In your bed
In the morning so still

VII

If you were alive today, madala –
I'd buy you a suit and soft skin ostrich shoes
I'd fly you to Durban or Cape Town
So you could walk on the beach
Feel the soft grains of summer sand
I'd take you out to sit down restaurants
Try out shrimps, mussels and this good food I eat

If you were alive today, madala –
We would plant avocado and litchi trees
Grow spinach and beetroot together
Pinch and prune sweetest tomatoes that yield
You would teach me how to dig a trench
How to prepare a seedbed for seedlings
How to make ridges and furrows
How to mulch and make compost and manure
How to save water and use grey water
We would grow those red roses
And maintain those white lilies
We would do gardening on our ancestral land
Singing your song:

7/8 u ya lithanda isaka la mazambani
U ya lithanda isaka la mazambani

If you were alive today, madala –
You would tell me how you survived the white dog
That followed you every morning to work
The dog that would run fast past you
The strange dog that would slide through your legs
Or even hit your legs with its tail
The dog that walked ahead of you
The dog that numbed your feet
The dog that shook and wearied your bones
The dog that disappeared at the bus stop
Just before the hospital gate
The same white *vaveni* that received you back from work
But couldn't enter the gate to your house
To throw you into a grave

If you were alive today, madala –
You would tell me about that rope
That roamed in your nightmares
The rope that made you so impatient
And hate everything about your wife
The rope that made you hit her
And want to kill her with a knife
The rope that prophet Muvhangeli said:
Don't pick it up when you find it placed on your path
The tough rope of wicked relatives
Who had long sized your neck

If you were alive today, madala –
You would tell me how you and Ngholeni picked up that dead rabbit
Early in the morning on your way to work
How you skinned the rabbit with delight

73

How you wanted to cook it for lunch
When suddenly a strange man came
And touched your forehead
And said: *and hi yena papantsongo wa Frank.*
Then your forehead ached and pounded
And when you came back home from work
The same strange man
Hobbled to your house
All he said was one sentence:
I needed to find Frank's brother's place
Then he vanished
Stealing your heart
Placing it in a cave
Planting a cockerel's heart in you
And you coughed and coughed

*

Papa, I know it took us twenty years to erect your tombstone
All along the wind was blowing you away
The sun was burning you
Your pillow was your hand
But now Bila, Mhlahlandlela, rest in peace
Do not open the grave and come home wearing shorts
Since you left, your wife has remained in the house
I've not seen a man sitting on your chair
It's still your house
Full of trees and vegetables

7/8 u ya lithanda isaka la mazambani
U ya lithanda isaka la mazambani

Baba Mandela

You're nothing if you offer no resistance.
Live as though your soul itself were of flesh.
Plant your feet firmly, for the times are bad
– from "If You Offer No Resistance" by Mihaly Babits

We overwork you our slave martyr,
For we are a fettered spirit.
When you say you are retiring from retirement,
We simply don't listen.
Instead we scream how much we need you.

We drag you old bandiet to extinguish blazing fires
In exploding war swamps – in disease decaying villages.
Silky deadly corporate mambas hide their stinking tails behind you.
Hasty media crews bulldoze you to make endless statements.
They have deadlines to meet – profits to rake.

Cameras click & beep non-stop even when you cough.
We push and shove each other when you drive past,
Even nameless wolves & bears with crude claws leap towards you.
Some young women fantasise taking you to the shower.
The small currency will plummet when you finally go.

You've been the voice of the voiceless
In the condemned cold cell & in this uneven world of today.
Throughout your life you've struggled
To diminish the demon of racism.
But murderous corporates have become larger than life.

You've made statements miles ago;
Even against the wrathful Bush's gassing of Afghanistan and Iraq.

You've refused to shake Bush's steel-cold hand in your poverty-
  gripped land,
Let him go back to his blood-stained white house in his United
  Snakes of Amnesia,
We cannot watch greed tug down humanity for oil ceaselessly

We fly you to Zurich for our World Cup bid.
When you enter the hall ...
Smartly-dressed handsome tall man walking on stick,
Proud harbinger of peace, bone-tired yet unbent justice warrior
Blatter & the rest rise and clap for the black saint.
Without you, this world is a desert –
A caged bird with a wounded voice.
You shed a tear wordlessly,
I cry instantaneously.

"The 2010 World Cup will be organised in South Africa,"
Delighted Blatter announces.
Hurray! I am a patriot too.
The elite's taste buds are already wet.
Without you, we have nothing to boast about
In our ravaged African dreams.

Baba Mandela, you've welded and mended us *nearly* together.
Have you ever proclaimed yourself a Marxist-Leninist or Maoist?
Can I demand socialism from your burdened shoulders?
Tortured souls like you must walk in the woods and meadowlands.
Spring is longing for you. Listen to the carefree singing bird.
Gather grandchildren, tell them fables and tales
As you sip mageu and digest Handel and Tchaikovsky.

Baba Mandela,
Even after retirement and hurricane marriage,

Even after you've been granted the freedom of City Johannesburg,
Still, you cannot walk the streets of free South Africa freely,
Without those cold heavily-armed bodyguards...
Disgusting...
What kind of freedom is ours?

You say you are ready to go to the grave,
Join friends in the other peaceful world.
What do you mean Baba Mandela?
To leave us orphaned?
What more do we want from you Baba Mandela?

The toilet cleaner at OR Tambo International Airport

Young and energetic
with a clean-shaven head
and well-trimmed beard
and red work wear
smiles broadly:
"Good afternoon sir,
welcome to my office."
Then he goes to the toilet cubicle, cleans it,
kills the odour of any diarrhoea
with detergents

The man in the urinal
wearing an expensive black suit
executive tie and pointed shoes –
the man who pushes a black suitcase
full of modern gadgets, cash, credit cards,

important documents and perhaps a bottle of whisky
this familiar black diamond says:
"You have a nice office man!"

He bursts into uncontrollable laughter
Hahaha! Hahaha! Hahaha!
Hehehe! Hehehe! Hehehe!
Kekeke! Kekeke! Kekeke!
Wakakaka! Wakakakakaaa!
Wakakakakakaaaaaaa!
Wakakakakakakakaaaaaaa!

See explanatory notes for "In the name of Amandla" and "Ancestral wealth" at the end of the anthology.

Bulelani Zantsi

The clan names of amaBhele

I am a child of the amaBhele clan
Of the Dlambulo, of the Khuboni
Of the Qunta, of the Mafu
Of the Langa, of the Mnomana
Of the Mbutho, of the Ncana
Of the Ntanda, of the Mbikazi
Of the Ndabezitha, of the Madiba clan

When I present myself to you I first build a highway with the ancestors:

We are the amaBhele of the household of Khuboni
Who praise ourselves with the sun of Langa's name
The household of the Ntandas who love to be raised
The household of the Mbikazis – the really *very* ugly ones
But a person who is totally unattractive should not be discarded
It is they who milk for their children even while it snows
It is they who smooth out the road, who even patch the potholes
Yes, they have buttocks so beautiful they can be kissed
It is easy to tell if someone is a young blue-blooded amaBhele
So tough is he that when cooked together with stones
The stones will be soft before the blue-blooded amaBhele
They are the ones who eat the cob with their in-laws
At Noqumbulo's place
They are like a buffalo who escapes from hunters even when mortally
    wounded
They rather eat the entrails of a wild beast than that of a placid cow
Awu! Awu! I am scared to brey the leather too energetically
For fear that it tatters and weakens
So that is how it is, all of us; we in this constellation of the living
    and the living dead.

Praise-singers of the house of Ntu

Awu! Which are the words to begin with, young uncircumsized men?
Let me dare to step into the unformed landscape
And to shape my tongue well as I am hailing the initiators
   of the Xhosa,
I will be like the bush-shrike, a bird with extensive activities
My sweeping efforts will commence like the wings of the vulture.
Silence please, for the imbongi from Vulture-hill to bellow.
Those wretches stumbling along like emaciated cattle must be quiet
As I am about to speak of matters tremendous and serious.
I shall speak in the deep Xhosa of Xhosaland.
I shall speak it until some are wholly edgy like liars,
Those who stir everywhere like red rhebuck in a thunderstorm.
I will call out clearly like a songbird against the stony mountain.

Praise singers, lend me two bush-tiger capes.
I shall gird myself with one and with the other sweep the way clear.
You fellows there, lend me two fighting sticks.
I shall take one to the gathering and with the other strike at weeds.
New initiates, lend me two crook-hilt knives.
I shall slaughter for the ancestors with one and with the other slice
   reams of meat for the elders.
Circumsized men, lend me two wild-olive staffs.
I shall tame wild animals with one and with the other drive off the
   thunder.
Young men, lend me two dancing canes.
I shall give one to the crane-feather heads and with the other beat
   against my shield.
Women, lend me a string of words.
I shall call out restoration from the abundance thereof and praise
   Qamata with the rest.
All hail to you, most praiseworthy ones.
Do not pinch the winged termite by the head while it is still emerging

80

from the ground.
Collect the sunlight now! The sun will go back to its mother, you
  children of the old black kraal-dung.
The Xhosa say that the calves should be driven home while it is still light.
Cover your grip around the fighting stick with cloth, be ready for
  those who have been beaten with a noisy but harmless set of
  sugar canes.
Thus I call you the calves that can shoot the bee-catcher bird with an
  arrow up on the mountain.
Condemn the cleft-lip to the people of old and thrust your fingers at
  the insincere.
Do not grab the pigeon by the tail-feathers, or your footsteps will
  become muddled.
Gird yourselves with capes of wild hides and be true.
Take up spears and let your strong forearms lead you on the way.
At the pure-bred place of Tshiwo you must wear sandals, because
  the ground is rough.
Leave me to get off the stage, because I speak freely until I get a lid
  put on.
Hayi, Yo-o-o! Let me give it all up!

*Translated from the Xhosa by Sindiwe Magona, JC (Koos) Oosthuysen
and Antjie Krog.*

Bongekile Mbanjwa

Lock and key

I am a broken pot,
I am the walking dead.
Where are my origins?
Where is the favourite, KaZulu?
Where is the pot, Zulu?

With what is winter porridge going to be stirred?
Where is it going to be stirred?
Who is going to eat it?
They are wandering in the ridges,
They are walking up and down
Searching for 'western' life,
Searching for the destroyer of the land.

What are we offering to the young generation?
What will generations to come pride themselves about?
We are like bats really.
I am crying for grandmothers and grandfathers
Who will be called to account by the ancestors.
I say: Where are you son of Mbuli?
I say: Your voice should shout out!
Nation, grandchildren of Zulu,
You shouted in front and I was sober.
I heard you with my own ears Mzwakhe
When the sun went down.

Ho! He! Now where are you?
The lion's paws have gripped you tight.
They snapped you tight and there was silence.

They locked you inside dark cells.
I say: Where are you ancestral spirits?
I say: Why are you silent when our valuables disappear?
We grope in the dark, my father's child.
The key is lost.

Why?

I have had enough of digging.
I searched, and was tired.
I asked and asked again,
But no one gave me the answer.
Why?

The cow's teat is full of milk
But there is no bucket,
So where are we going to store it?
Let it not turn to curds
Before the young generation can eat and finish up!

Milk-pail, where can we find you?
Milk-pail, how do we find you?
Milk-pail, who can find you?
Whose children will enjoy you?
If things go on like this
We shall be left sucking our thumbs.

Day and night wasps are buzzing.
I take pen and paper and write.
I write again and again

But curds end up in my fingers
Because I do not have the milk calabash.
Who can find it?

I thought about discriminating according to race
But disagreed.
We have our heroes who have the milk pail
Where we can guzzle.

Why don't they open the gate for us to enter?
Why are they not breaking these chains?
What are we going to leave for the generations to come?
I will not stop asking:
Why?

Translated from the Zulu by Siphiwe ka Ngwenya.

ARI SITAS

Slave Trades (extracts)

1.

I had them strap a seat and lift me up
my body swelling, rotting in the sun
and march me down the twisted, acrid paths
to take me down to sea.

They shall count us after the flood and we shall still be two
I thought
After the flood we shall be counted two by two
I thought
but deep inside I knew that Africa had all its wiser ways
and on the road, the bone and shrub cut deep inside my soul

They shall count us one by one astride our lonely beds
or else they shall not find us when the counting starts
and we shall dwindle off with just our putrid breathing
and cut the landscape up
              not with our plough, or flower or heart
                   but with an axe.

2.

I saw him lifted up, his face – flabby, loose, distended
his songs long forgotten,
lost in the fevers of his infernal sorrows
and his shroud, lean, threadbare and his colonies of slaves
sinking in the mud

his dreams floating down, down towards the Red Sea
his soft parts pulped, reeking the foulest of desires
and his hide – only a fish's sheen
his sheen a fish's scent.

His hirelings buckled under his weight
edging forward
a funerary bulk
moving past the ostrich's, the camel's, darting, bluegrey eyes.

3.

I remember most of all his hands, large, larger than language,
stubborn hands, sturdier than a Harari horse
and his spoor of stale garlic, of ever-reeking sweat
plastered up in perfume
and his flannel underwear, I do remember grimy and his eyes
darting out haunted by the steps of perky Arab boys

I remember his hands and the gift of whiteman's disease and
semen in my loins
and he laughed at me – "you truly believe in God?" he used to tease
as he held on to twist my nipple
holding the writ that made me his

for eighty guns,
        between his legs.

4.

Come here, follow me past the markets of Addi-Abbi
past my ancestral homes

where the older gods stirred thunderclouds with vengeance
and where the new one hammered on wood is
guarded by shrill, austere monks and parchment
come, here, look at the footprints
and the marks all creatures formed as traces in the mud
here: come, the zebra stumped a hoof and here: a lioness and
cubs have littered here
come, follow me down to the canyon's forked fingers
that point you down and shove you down to my valleys
look: left, the Semien range – pink, pink from all the snow
and the harsh sunrays of my ancestral gods and later,
as the sun sets you will see how it makes the clouds
around its nose look like dark clerical hats on fire
now red, now redder, now redfire-coloured.

Slide down the little waterfall with me
the rainbow
in the trickle will not hurt you
here, run through the coffee garden
past the fruit-trees and the flowers
smell how my people cook the thick banana on open fires
look at these pomegranates, oranges, limes.

Come, let us run around the hill there
past the songs boys and girls intone
twist with me past the bank of the Taccuzze River
come, here, by the tall poplars
here, you see, some of the footprints stop
here is the clubbing ground
the dented skulls heaped up just there
are of the ones who
were too lame to make it to the sea
to fetch a price, come, follow me,
see how the weather made them, how it makes them shine.

5.

Give me the moon she said not knowing that I hated women and their petted cages, their canaries and the lice they grew in their marvellous rose gardens; I would have never reached for the moon for her, for them.

They never understood that deep inside the hues that the sun makes to dazzle on the water, on the wave which is cut in twos by my dream-armadas, by my brainfins of a shark, all my images of them have been stark, maternal, barren.

She never understood that she paced around my house as ornament and sphinx for others; and I was kind with my love for her, I was kind with my affection and my counsel; but she frowned and despaired and when at night, after her first sobs and prayers, trembling and pleas, after boiling the sea water for drinking in this parched, desperate, nothing of a town, she spun a web around our bed and I sunk into my purgatory year.

I did not treat her like all the others do to her own kind; I did not call her savage, brute and lice-infested wench; I did not place a chain around her neck and lead her down to market; to the growls of the surrounding town and folk I made her the princess of my sand-infested, cow-dung polished dorms.

I fought for silk and thread for her in every market; I traded wines and grapes for ornamental gold; I unloaded camel hordes of rifles for her chamber's sheets; I paid in kind for years to get her taught the French ways, to hold her own. But she paced up and down my inner courtyard like a demented whore.

I did not come to this godforsaken place to dream, I did come to kill the dream, there was too much of it over there and much of it too soon.

She will be gone with florins round her neck, back to her tribesmen.

She will be gone because I cannot make her mine, and through my doorstep or outside in this treeless dump, no one else will make her his no more.

She will be gone from the records of our life and those who will remember her have not even learnt her name.

She will walk the three rows of mudhouses to the port in the early morning and the wind will resand her footprints on the path.

She will be referred to as this girl who lived with him, almost his wife, for almost one year; this tall, slim, light-coloured beauty with her matted hair who did not succumb to the Mission School's grind, who wore him out; the stupid native, who lacked the intelligence to be his bride; damn it, yes the woman he abandoned because he chose the adventurer's and the corsair's life.

I looked at her and said: farewell Eva, go.

She looked at me and frowned, turned and let Africa's magnet tag her in, away and in, and into the landscape of all of my despairs.

I am the she, whose centre disappears
I am not
I am unwritten

unclassified
I am the last murmur of something older
than chattel or rifle
I am the dangerous she
unbaptised
exposed without purdah
uncircumcised
bought for guns, but unpriced
unsaved from the serpent
with too many odours to be formed by a magician's brush
unlineaged, suspended in memory
dispossessed of any line that roots me aground in the wind
ancient, not Evaed
Nobkhubulwana knows my name
Athena knows my black name
When I play my harp
sonnets kill like arrows:

"I saw them coming to my homestead crying
their bare breasts stiffened from fear
hide us, they begged
you can have a score of the best spotted cattle
do not let us be taken by your Christian friends
give us genitals and clothes so we can be seen
as weak men and tie our breasts down so our chests
feel just flat and wobbly
hide us and we will give you the very first yam crop
the dates and the nuts we have grown
let us be seen to be defective men
rather than women with active wombs
and loins that can squeeze out animals for branding
in the market of the believers."

I see him now, consumed against a crimson desert sky, beyond
hope or death returning to the eel-eating country of his birth. I
see my kin, shading their eyes with the guns my brother bought in
exchange for my firm backside.

And I scream at the scrawny birds of fate – I am the she they
cannot centre, I am the unshe of their nightmares, I am the
footstomping, ever flowering mother of my ever thirsting rib and
torso and wing.

6.

Love me, protect me and trust me he said; but I had to go, to flee
and he didn't like it, like we don't like pacing around all places
where love had died

Please come back to me, and I miss you and all such trifles were
his romantic daily fare, pathetic as he fussed over every hint of
me and cried and cried

Look I am kissing your letters, I am eating your rhymes, ironing
your clothes, shining your moccasin shoes, combing your hair, I
love you I said but I lied

I am me, me all yours, all you for me, all here, he shrieked,
drunk, hysterical, refusing to accept that indeed he was dead, a
nothing, a well that had dried

My white, black redwhite lover, bled black
be gone, stand back

I will be leaving your city, look at its kindness, its shadows, look
at its officers of the law with cardboard wings erected on their
backs, look at their lives

Your whores with tin-haloes, obese from too much bile and food,
look how they hang their garters off the moon, look at them
rattle too, the noise you call love-music in your cruel hives

Look at your drain-unclogging workmen look what cancers they
pull off your rats' hair, look at their handbones crumble, warp
and burn, look at them circumcise themselves with their blunt
knives

My white, black, redwhite lover, bled black
be gone, stand back

I will leave the crumbling church wall far behind, your bourgeois
magic further still, your fetid smells and worn out suits, your
many tremors of the flesh and moans

I will not rest in some rural dale, with our pale sun adrift, alone,
lamenting the perfume of lost loves, the hazes that your voice
out-drones

be gone, stand back

I will be the dancer on a sea so thick, thicker than wine or a pond
so thickset and dark by a scented town so thirsty for my porous
exile, so deep that it holds no memories of the drowned, the dead,
the slave, the knife, the black angel's versifiers so grey that it
forgets the sun. And You.

Keorapetse Kgositsile

Affirmation

The sound of her voice
weaves a song with meaning
past the depths of any word
that might try to name
or bridle and tame it

In the sound of her voice
I remember every thing
I will never forget

Love might not be all
that a person needs
but it does count

Here with my little hand upon
the tapestry of memory and my loin
I once again lean on the blues to find voice:
if loving you is wrong
I don't want to do right.

No boundaries

I possess neither wings
nor the magician's mischief
but, believe me, I can fly
and I can also be a landscape

of mirrors that name whatever moves
or has pretensions to be alive

On the wingspan of my desire
easy as the approach of any day
you can clearly remember
I can fly to any place
or moment fertile with memory
or create fresh ones without a single boundary
though our lives remain so pathetically prosaic

With informed hope
and resolve we must know
how to move forward to a landscape
where our dreams cannot be turned into nightmare
where our dreams are always in sight
where we must again
redden the blackest folds
of our memory and intent

Renaissance

I remount the curve of evil times
to unearth my anchored memory
– Abdellatif Laabi

Again I say
I am music people
the cadence of what
we are moved by and move to

informs my eye
which does not want to risk
even a blink
for fear I might miss

some essential gesture
of the life we must live
in all its robustness
and sing as ours here
or any where we choose
breaking through all the silences
in the crevices of our turbulent memory

soundman
that I have always aspired to be
my ear sees the tentacles
of our fragile voice
breaking through the walls of our exiles
as I remount the curve of evil times
to unearth my anchored memory

Mongane Wally Serote

Freedom, Lament and Song (extract)

remember
the honesty of history is and can be cruel
it is also
it is also a song, it is footsteps
history is you and me
history is day and is night
history is how you fought to lift a hand
and how to put it down
history is history
in the heart of a worker
in the head of a worker
and a man
and a woman
history is the birth of a child
history is the death of a child
history is that which happens
that which is repeated
and done
and through time and
history
because it is like the seasons
it repeats itself like a reflection
in your eye
in my eye
when i see me in you
and you in me in my eyes
history makes and unmakes life and time
speaks
listens

it is the morning minute
which we push and must intervene
shift
which we witness which changes you and me
as we know
it did
history is the heavy hour arm
history is the light minute arm
to the small second
is you and me
history is no similar minute
or hour or second
history is now when it's no more
history ends when it ends
if it ends
history is the old lady of the bolshoi
who intervenes
and the little girl learning ballet
it is the woman who dances
spins and swings
propels and flies
in a dance
in the air and space
it is the will
it is the altitude
it is you
history is a dance of the muscle
of the body on the air
on the heart
it is the body and the dance on the air
history flies like light
it is time
it flies like an eagle in the blue space
in the swift and smoke air

it pounds
it dances and flails
it flies, swings and spins
like time
like the earth
like day and night
history makes time and you and me
history is like science
is like technology which embraces knowledge to use it
it shapes things
it shapes the brains and faces
it is a story
history exists at the beginning of time
and enters at its end
history speaks and glides in speech
when time ends it starts
and when it ends time begins with human intervention
history i said
is hard like steel
is soft like the glide of a vulture
history
is my story and i speak of it
i tell my story
remember history
history is the Zairean dance
is the Ghanaian dance
history is the Angolan dance
and the township dance
history is the Mozambican dance troupe
no matter the size of war
no matter the size of the sound of the war
no matter the size of the explosive package
the dance troupes
the dancers are here to continue the dance and dance

they are the size of life they dance
here we go again, they survive life
the song and history, says
here
life says, we go again.

JEREMY CRONIN

End of the century – which is why wipers

Let's leave pessimism for better times
– spray-painted on a wall in Bogota

1.

With windscreen wipers
(Unlike drive-belts
Or footwear, or chameleons' tongues)
Low adhesion is advised.

But for this end of century
Wipers should be given
Some additional stickiness
Some adhesive stubbornness   to turn
Grand vision into rhythm
    Light into rubber
        Narrative into epigram

These being more useful inclinations, I think
At this end of a bad millennium

2.

Some time after the revolution, Soviet libraries adopted the Dewey
Decimal System

With one rectification – the two hundreds: Religion

All the way from 201, 202, 214 (Theodicy), 216 (Good & Evil), 229
(Apocrypha & pseudo-epigraphs), down to 299 (Other religion) –
this great textual body of human wisdom, confusion,
folly and aspiration was reduced by the Soviets to a bald:

Dewey Decimal 200: Atheism

This was not (not by far) the worst sin of Stalinism

But it was its most typical

This should be remembered of the 20th century

3.

I decline to name my windscreen wipers
"Easy Come" and "Easy Go",
I think of them, rather, as
"Quote" and "Unquote"

Between them
Reality
Lies in parenthesis

4.

Clandestine communist cells were organised
Right inside of the Nazi death camps
(Each one   a parenthesis)

Cell members used cigarettes to bribe camp officials, to get messages
out, obtain medicine in,

or to win space to perform this or that other small task of
solidarity and survival

A condition for secret Party membership was the payment of a weekly
sub – one cigarette

Somehow to be stolen from the guards

How many militants were summarily executed?

How many were caught trying to meet the brave challenge of stealing
the week's levy?

This, too, should not be forgotten of our century

5.

I name my wipers:

"On the One Hand", and
"On the Other Hand"

6.

Those who lost the Cold War
Did not deserve to win   in the end

Those who won the Cold War
Were (and are) entirely
Unworthy of their triumph

7.

I am very much worried, ma-comrades, I mean if we get
retrenched, or contracted out, or sent to i-casualised ward, is
because why?

Soren-so says for economic growth we have to via global
competitiveness, by so saying

i-Management says, workers, the ball's in your court

We have given you, they say

A good package

(Which is almost the same phrase Kgalema had just used with irony,
thirty minutes before, as we waited for this very meeting with FAWU
shop-stewards)

(Which meeting eventually started two hours late)

(Which is why we'd been watching soccer on TV in a breakaway
room, and I was distractedly trying also to write a poem about the end
of the century, while Steve Lekoelea looped in a weak cross that was
easily cut out by Chief's defence)

And Kgalema said – "No,

It was a good pass

Just to the wrong team"

And I thought: That's it!

That could be the poem about the end of the 20th century

   8.

In the shadow of the big banks   a stokvel
Home brew   in the backyard

In a thump of rubber   with the foot
To wake up your ancestors   in a mine-compound
With a gumboot dance

For most of this century
People's cultures have retreated to the secret
Thaba Bosius of the soul

Forced to stratagems of non-hegemony –
Rhythm, syncretism, exhibition for the tourist, slant-wise to reality

But what went up to the high plateaux as wedding song, or
   hunting chant
Came down, sooner or later, transformed

In a factory choir, or toyi-toyi on the street
And is even now an incalculable resource to go, bravely
Slant-wise, into this next imperial century

9.

With all the ambivalence of a car in the city

Being of the street and

Not of it, just passing through

Down Tudhope, wipers at work, rubber-thump, rubber-thump,
    taking the bend in the shadow of the tower blocks, then, where
    the next bend sweeps left

Just there

One day   it's an inner city father walking his four-year-old kid
    to creche

One day   a kerb-side telephone hawker ("Howzit?", "No, grand")
    with her extension cord looping up to a jack in a third floor flat

One day   it's a bucket with "For Sale" (cooked sheep's trotters)
    "Johnny Walkers", they're called

One day   it's the crash-in-transit Toyota that I see first

Then the polaroid photographer, then the taxi-driver himself

Posing, door open, left elbow on bonnet, tossing away a cigarette
    butt (one week's sub?), for a snap-shot to be sent to someone,
    somewhere (rural?), no doubt, else

This tenderness, make-do, wit, role-reversal, job-pride, all in the midst
    of a crumbling, an urban, end of century, something else

10.

The wisdom of windscreen wipers
Is velocity's blink
Hesitation in onward rush
An ironic side-swipe on the hypothetical free-way N1 North

In this end of millennium downpour

Where we've become habitual, edgy, typical, turned to a split-second hi

One of the genus: desperate whisk, squeegee, scull-oar, either/or

Wavering with intent

In this global, totalitarian, homogenised deluge, where parents, patients,
dependants, lovers, learners, supporters, congregants, citizens (if we
still exist) are zombified into one thing all – clients

And public (if they still exist) institutions are made, the leaner
the meaner the better, contractual service providers

Where managerialism is the ism to make all isms wasms, the new 200
Dewey Decimal, the delirium of our age

Which is why wipers

With their cantilevered, elegant, frenetic, rubber-thump, rubber-thump

Activism want to insist

Clarity of vision
Forward progress
Proceeding wisely to the point
Involve
A certain

On the one hand
On the other hand
Prevarication
As into
Another millennium
With its own impending
Miscellany, theodicy, good & evil, apocrypha
You/We
Either way, now
Slant-wise
Ironically
Plunge

Mxolisi Nyezwa

it all begins

it all begins with thunder in the middle of the road,
it begins with people bleeding from the intestine –
it begins with one statement,
with the scratch of one pen.
it begins with the smell of death dying
with people of all sizes in every epoch
shouting from the grave.

it begins with the man in the personnel department,
it begins with the smell of frying eggs
the brief passage and elongation/reflux of time,
on the contrary –
it begins with the promise of peace
in the avalanche of lies.

and it could be all these things
as it yawns in the morning
with the blunder bearing on us
with the emergence of summer
the fire of history closes its doors behind us
and sunk geniuses walk about
aimlessly through the air –

and it all begins
and it will never cease.

Story

i live east of the city
near the violent sea
like all good men
i was crazed from birth

in the homes
with poor children
my simple story
runs like this

in the city
near the sea
i live alone
like a humble man
who cares for others

far away
under the sun
and the luminous sky
my house is built
in the rain

i fear midnight

in the nearby township
light fades
in a hurry
like wild seeds
in the sun.

Songs from the earth

i live in a township
in a small red house
next to a shebeen
and a volcanic school
with sad teachers
my woman laughs
all day long
and makes the porcelain dish weep
while a heavy stone
thunders in my forehead
and from every tree
and every branch
dismal songs from the earth
cries of tormented deaths
flash violently
in the sky
like the furious smell
of drugs in the street
or at times
like the roasting
of basalt leaves.

Letters of demand

i'm getting letters of demand from unlikely places
all my investments and insurance policies
that i commenced
with a student stipend
have suddenly expired
in the smoking country
and all my worries of yesterday
are immediately brought up today
like a smile
all the embraces the handshakes
the understanding gestures
return to me uncomfortable
and blue

soon acquaintances will look at me and hurry away
towards the hanging cliff
next to van stadens bridge
those who chase me from their toilets
and their treasure domes
have seconded my name
to the president
as literary advisor
from a province
that only reads
when there is a murder
or when somebody
breaks savagely
with an axe
a citizen's skull.

The road ahead

don't ask me about any of my poems
for i will tell you that people are murdered in my country
and their deaths arrive slowly as an illness
as a desolate knock
on a blank sky

i wear my shoes in the morning like i'm in a hurry for something
the tea-cup rests on the table, its shadow long and tapering
everywhere the fruit gives golden or red sulphur
what has become of us?
what has become of us?

how do i say this, that once your eyes

how do i say this, that once your eyes were like topaz
and your heart clean as jasmine
in the dense forests i follow the black traces of your lashes
in the empty memory of lost time
my feet tumble against cold hope

you who have cast the first stone
and robbed my blithe existence of its foliage
i walk bearing like death
the heavy punch of your eyes
the eyelashes of your smile.

they have asked me many times

they have asked me many times about my poems
and what makes my heart grow softer than lightning
in all the years in New Brighton
i have written down simple words
to trace the movement of the stars

inside these fiery walls a momentary blue is discerned
you are now naked as vinegar and garlic
we cannot be together triumphant in this world
bread and salt on our table
joined by a thirsty hunger.

ISABELLA MOTADINYANE

Nonhlanhla

Nonhlanhla is gone
tears pearls laughter
dreads survey my toes
touch of anguish
pat my mind
the target is found
Nonhlanhla is gone
they nailed her
pink nails oozing
they dragged her
reshuffled her
off the ground
pinned her tongue
hanging loose
blood pool flooded
to dry up heavens
Nonhlanhla is gone
staring
into the dark
tired of nkosi yami
go away
biting my lips
my dark room walls
caressing the belt
to end the beginning
of a faraway song
in my mind
Zion bells ring
bayavuya umoya wami

uyakathazeka
voices crying
in the dark
darkness
swallows the light
my heart
has stopped beating
no mercy in Zion
Nonhlanhla is gone

Red crown

A cry
of come and see
our home is a home
of tears and bitterness
women crying
night and day
a black cockerel
red crown
is in the house
a smash hit
mother father child
ending up with
an infant
it started
with a dog outside
a cry
of come and see
what can we do now
household and furniture

everything is gone
we found a woman
in tears inside
a crying mother
is now a song

Come people

Paaha
come people
Paaha
come people
it is time to do away with weeds
it is time for the harvest
come let us talk
come in peace
Paaha
come people
Paaha
come people
it is summer time
the corncob is mature and ripe
have you ever heard
news of happiness?

Sink a shaft

Dark night babe
toss and turn
the clouds above
you make the sober go drunk
come in from the cold
warm you up
sink down our throat
the clouds above
mountain so high
sink babe sink
sink a shaft
move slowly down the mountain
down our throats
toss and turn babe
sink on me
all night
in dark nights clouds above
you make the sober go drunk
sink babe sink
sink it smooth
sink a shaft

Translated from the Sotho and isicamtho by Ike Mboneni Muila.

GERT VLOK NEL

Beautiful in Beaufort West

& you were beautiful in Beaufort West and I was so frightened and so
amazingly in love with you & you & I had sex on graves & on trains &
on the back seats of Ford Fairlanes now you and your husband are both
computer analysts & last winter you tried to cut both your wrists &
now you can't sleep anymore, can't laugh anymore, can't do anything for
yourself, will never kiss me again

& your words were beautiful beautiful beautiful also when you were
smoking menthol cigarettes and said those sweet sweet things to me
while you lay sweet sweet in my arms & I've totally forgotten the exact
words I only remember the smoke & the sweat in Beaufort West &
your naked body under a cool cotton summer dress can't sleep anymore,
can't laugh anymore, never do anything for each other again, never kiss
each other again

& maybe it's like a story from a woman's magazine, but one evening
you suddenly pushed me away & looked at your face in the rear view
mirror & said "maybe I should look happier" that evening I just
couldn't get to sleep & the feeling that my heart would tear right out of
my body & like a rowboat that's floating away on the river I could not
sleep anymore, not laugh anymore, not do anything right again, never
kiss you again

& the last memory I'll sing about is the night when you and I rode
the milk train one-to-one into the night to the other side of the ding
dong gong of the breakfast waiter passing in the corridor & this was
my wake-up call my love, you said "please love me" but I dreamed that
we went to live in Beaufort West & I couldn't sleep anymore, couldn't
laugh, couldn't just do something like that, will never kiss you again

River

River O River you're the deepest word I know
I could navigate by you to the sea & to her in the hope
that I would win her heart, but desert is the word
by which I must journey to win her heart

Last night I slept in Pretoria
in the wrong city with the wrong woman
which now means that I must journey to you in the Cape with my hat
in my hand through the most frightening country
O my Darling, can you hear me there where you're sleeping?

Last night I slept in Bloemfontein
was happy I had got so far in one day was happy
there were still flowers for hikers to pick (wanted to call you)
was happy love will not pass me by was happy
it's only another 1000 km
from the Cape

Last night I slept in Colesberg
across from the garage where the trucks that bring the prostitutes
turn
& hiking back to the Cape in the long night
I saw some
crying I saw others singing maybe about the
mixed feelings you get
from turning things around

Last night I slept in Beaufort West
in the Wagon Wheel Motel wanted to call you
say that I am dreamless
fistless world-weary & have had enough &
want to come and sleep with you forever & it's only another
500 km from the Cape

Hillside lullaby

I live here in the town where the trains whistle
& the shunters shift the trains around on tracks
day & night
& I'm very much all right
do you remember when you were going to live with me...
how did our story go from there?
trains that shunt, trains that stay
trains that always ride in circles here

dream of me & leave me free tonight

this morning early there was a loud bang
down there on that side of the railway bridge
but everything was very much all right
it's only me I long for you so much
& in the meantime everything frightens me
all the words lie empty in my hand
because my heart sleeps with you
where the trains shunt.

dream of me & leave me free tonight

leaving behind the beautiful words of Beaufort West

my Uncle Jakkie was as old as I am one dead still evening when his
face was suddenly distorted in the bathroom mirror
like a word spelt wrong and he fell straight over backwards his full
   length

in my granny's cramped little bathroom in Nuwe Straat 166 Beaufort
    West like a page
blown over in the year of 1978 in the kitchen next door granny was
    already in her flannel nightdress
grandpa in an adjectiveless hangover and Uncle Goegie in whatever
since words had already begun to tragically fail Uncle Goegie kicked the
    bathroom door
open without an adverb Uncle Jackie was as naked and dead as all words
and he'd pissed himself granny shrieked grandpa somethinged
and so everyone left Beaufort West in kisses and seasons for Dixi
and left behind beautiful words that started to become all the more
    unbeautiful
but in the beginning was the word and the word was with Beaufort West
and the word was Beaufort West and the word was beautiful

Why I'm calling you tonight

GERT above the ground calling Koos beneath the ground come in
    Koos come in
WHY I'm calling you tonight it's a dark evening deep in the month
    of july
AND it's been raining all day long on the cellphone masts and
    telephone lines between here & your grave in the word transvaal and I
    let your nicest record fall off the hi-fi

KOOS the line is dead between my heart & your mouth's most
    beautiful words
AND between your words and resorts where the far wind blows &
    where have the ships in the bay gone to
ALL the words have changed in the palm of our hand & now this is
    a strange land

SO sail slowly slowly all ye ships of the night from malta to mumbai
to deliver Koos's last words goo'bye Koos goo'bye goo'bye

KOOS I guess I'm saying goo'bye for good and above all forever
AND for the tent between the blue of stars and sapphires like
beaufort's air & the tough poems on your last loose papers
YOU were long my blackest troubadour you stirred the troubled
water of my troubled heart
BUT I know my heart was really then still coldwateromoclean
enough for the Lord and Tintin to live in
AND I could still sing in the month of march & I could still hear
deep trains shunting down at the railway yard
AND in the morning before school when I was squeezing pimples
in the mirror at ten to seven I could still see my soul in my eyes and
my whole life
AND the Gamka river wooshed through to the sea and at night the
13-up and 7-down train swished to the Cape and in such a night I
passed away

SO MUCH so that I was frightened when I saw in the yard that it
was a midday in march but the lights were all on in the street
shantih Koos shantih shantih

KOOS after you there were other Kooses who could also cry
beautifully in afrikaans
THERE was the cleverest Koos with a handful of fairy tales grim &
gay & he said look I write with my body my name is Koos & I am
like a sick rose
BUT he died a horrible death like a sunflower & sunflowers die
horribly

AND unceasingly through the night the most beautiful Koos drifted
to the east with the river as black as label through the night as black
as bible right to the magnificent word of the morning

AND also my friend Koos from beautiful west one night he jumped
the midnight train in a tuxedo on the impulse of the winter
midnight streetlight smalltown rain among other things tonight he
lies buried in Springs
KOOS show them please where they are to pitch their tents in the
milky way in that pitch dark goodnight Koos goodnight goodnight

YOU however were bullshitless Koos illusionless styleless dreamless
timeless groupyless wireless and totally hopeless
YOUR songs were so heart-wrendingly beautiful too beautiful too
beautiful to live in
THEY don't belong in Africa or hereabouts your songs don't belong
anywhere really
THROUGH the train window I see the midnight sun or is it a bit of
sun on the platform at Germiston station. I overslept in the train &
in the night I rode past my hometown & the house where I could
have poured out my heart
THE old hometown looks the same as you step down from the train
and there's your ma & your pa & mary down the lane but when
you stick your hand out they start to disappear.
WITH the years everything has unravelled Koos even your ma's deal
table
AND there's a song of yours whose words I can't remember
anymore
AND I don't know if you ever read a Tintin book but Tintin in
Tibet is the only book that Tintin ever cried in goodbye, Chang,
goodbye goodbye

IT was eleven o' clock at night on the late night news read by
blomerus niewoudt & I had just got home when my ma told me
that you
like Herman on the 45th cutting off-ramp into Durban in a
volkswagen beetle
had died that you

had wanted to drive to Nick's place to go and say something stupid
    even though they were already all in bed for god's sake that you
were sober and clear-headed that it
was high summer that the
night was so beautiful so beautiful that it
was the kind of night that trains and words travel to die and be
    dismantled that among
ten thousand nights it was the perfect night to say goodbye because
    you'd already left everything to Irma Karien Karla & Mornay and
    me & Koos
allow us your fans to retrace your last sad steps & say goodbye to
    you forever
farewell Kosie farewell farewell
because we're gracelandless Koos no memphis tennessee for us
    because
on the night of 15 january 1984 at the no doubt predestined hour it
pleased the god of life and death to let you drive
over
a low-water bridge the volksie began to slip and plough in slow
    motion
through the tambookie grass and through
all those lonely places where you always went until against
a tree and your upper body through the windscreen onto the bonnet
    & against
the tree you
half-dreaming & half-suffering & half confessing things
your eyes saw this somewhere & that somewhere else & maybe
    Herman who
came into the bay on the deck of the Carian all sails & he greets you
    he hails he
laughs and waves and calls I've come to pick you up Koos all around
    the world from malta to bombay
and at the word bombay you
turned and said something to us that we couldn't hear because of

the presence
of the wind but it was something like wind find bind kind & then
you
saw the morning breaking cold and wordless Koos & you were
happy and suddenly you were free

MORE or less all of this I reconstructed on night shift duty
as a failed attempt at a last salute goo'bye Koos goo'bye goo'bye

KOOS you sang about women the sea & the mines & I sing about
women the sea and the trains
AND I still remember the night when I heard that you were dead
in january '84 the country was so full of fear but the night was
beautiful in beaufort west
IT was eleven o'clock that night read on the late night news by
blomerus niewoudt
& I had just got home when my ma said to me GERT & all the trains
stopped

Epitaph

Last night I dreamed that I was living in 1975 again, the year
when I was last happy. Then I came down the stairs to the kitchen
& poured myself some water it was so quiet in the house.
The best years are gone. Anyway, & then I dreamed that
I would one day live as far away from 1998 as possible.

Last year I dreamed that I was living in my own most beautiful
words again in my most beautiful village & that I was starting
to get healthy again. Then I woke suddenly & something wasn't
right I was so lost I wasn't in my own home.
The most beautiful words are gone. Anyway & then I dreamed
that I could one day live in a language as far away from Afrikaans
as possible.

In my boyhood I had a girl she was beautiful
beyond Afrikaans she could make my heart dance in pain all night
& she was somehow Gert's last stance. And then she dreamed
that she had gone to live in a body as far away from my body
as possible.
The loveliest love is gone. Anyway, then I dreamed
that I had gone to live as far away near her body & as far away
from my body as possible.

Somewhere I dreamed that I attended my own funeral
& Pa was there & Ma was there & all my loves like in my happiest
year. But the best was that this the best
was this that I bent down to the ground & kissed myself
on my own mouth.
The most beautiful dreams are gone. Anyway & then I dreamed
that I could live in a dream as far away from here & now
as possible

Last night I dreamed that I was living in 1975 again, the year
when I was last happy. Then I came down the stairs to the kitchen
and poured myself some water it was so quiet in the house.
The best years are gone. Anyway, & then I dreamed that
I will one day live in a country as far away from South Africa
as possible.

*All poems translated from the Afrikaans by Richard Jurgens except for
"leaving behind the beautiful words of Beaufort West" translated from the
Afrikaans by Mike Dickman.*

KOBUS MOOLMAN

Poem from a Canadian diary

I carry a geography of the dark
with me across oceans, frozen lakes,
mountains whiter than ice, where wind
contours a need urgent as flesh.
This dark, the dark I know,
that does not ever, even in the glare
of dreaming, leave me, this recognition
familiar and strange as any echo
returning white across a frozen sea,
this dark is you – as long as you,
like the dark, carry absence
in the shape I carry with me.
Everywhere. The geography of a heart
in two halves.

Two moons

There are two moons
in this sky tonight, this dark
hole with no sides.

Hold onto the steep earth,
decipher the meaning of the lights
at both ends of the darkness:

One the colour of milk
with its smell, the other red
and thirsty as a transfusion.

They come again

They come again, the dark birds of clamour.

Their heavy wings beat like blows upon an anvil, like blows
    upon a metal bar.

They choke and grind the coarse gears of their voices.

In the distance the setting sun is a dry furnace – a back-draft
    that sucks all the air
and light out of the world.

Only the small chime of silver bells can hold off the clamour.

Only the thin scent of a blue flower can push back the dark.

KELWYN SOLE

This is not autumn

This is not autumn:
the skies are doused
in aching blue
without respite

nights are colder
there is little cloud
to entice us
into warmth.

Queleas swarm
in flocks like
grasshoppers
no longer

each farm drowses
after its harvest,
and quiet descends
on a veld surrendered

to a seared brown
to crackling scurf
and the slow musk
of wood fires.

We travelled
with belief
on shining roads
to know the lives

of our compatriots,
their heartbeat.
But our own thoughts
change. There is

panic and eagerness loose in the world. Last night's hotel tv was
pregnant with praise singers. You feel asleep, during *education comes*
   through sport,
and I had no strength to touch the dial to release me from my vigil
alone with shy mice and the maudlin sound of tyres in love with tar.
There was a hint of lightning, a trance of rain, briefly, to the east:
then from the west a sifting in the dewless sand, grain on lonely grain:
from the south a dirge came for the lost herds of Cochoquas:
from the north a tintinnabulation of trumpets and applauding
   jewellery
as ancient powerful men wagged thick forefingers in admonition
just like those before them.

In Hillbrow the streets are shattered glass.
In Pretoria they mint reflecting coins to spy any threat approaching.
In Orange Farm and Khayelitsha, a furtive noise of bailing buckets.
In Richmond there is no one who dare recognise a neighbour.

Tomorrow we will forfeit ourselves again to the soothings
of clerics, their fantasies of blame and of redemption tricked out
in rainbow colours. Will drive past billboards crooning the idiom
of Herdbuoys and Azaguys. See more of bureaucrats
– a glacial indifference – young people grown slickly self-important
in offices
               vocal with assurances they cannot hope to keep
who find time to redeem their own mortgages
with down-payments of our patience.

                              Yet for now
a woman passes us and waves and can't stop grinning
with the promise of a house – at last – within her eyes.
A child muses, longing for a friend to share his prickling intellect.
An old man reclaims his land, ploughs the soil with the joyful
calloused foresight of all who carry seed. Bricks
seek mortar then resolve to transform themselves to buildings.
Girls in makgabis are sinuous hankering for one day love

as we stop in the exact centre of this journey,
a chrome and steel button
                              among mealiefields stubbling in all directions
with no map to tell us where to go
                                        – seek anywhere
a language of candour a signpost but are awake only
to the sad shunting of a train, somewhere in the distance;
or try to read a script of looping ants
devouring a sandwich.

There are riddles
that possess us

            that we fear to name, enraptured
with optimism, yet weighted down with our forefathers'
genetic tombstones still clogged inside our brains.
A plague of eloquence beguiles this world to posturing,
a misplaced sanctimoniousness of spring.
The air stinks of trouble. And myths proliferate.

New country

In the soft part of our palms,
in the clasp of our own hands,
hidden between the calluses and scars,
that's where we'll find our country.

The land

– You see my house.
You see my wife,
my children, my mealies
and my dogs? Yes, over there –
They say I am hiding in this forest.
They say I have gone back
to drinking with the animals.
But in the location I would be
no one. I would just be

that thing that they call unemployed.

I never meant to cross the river

Who is weeping bereft inside our yard?

O mother! Why can't you hear from me the endless rustling in my heart?

Yes I went with him to the river. Mother, I went along

but I never meant to cross the river.

You told me he had cattle. You told me his mother was your friend. Yet I found his smile a tricking, lazy thing that crawled across his lips.

His face is not a sun to rise each day above my sleeping. His hands were two chickens pecking at the hard seeds on my breasts. I told him to leave my mouth alone.

He said he had a condom. He said

O mother: I never meant to cross the river.

I said I want to go back home. I tried. My feet disobeyed me on wet pebbles. Mother, I tried to run.

Mother, help me. I am sore between my legs; I am sore all the way deep to my heart.

I try to tell you this and try to tell my aunts. Why will nobody hear me? Why do your gazes turn away?

My aunts shout: it's all your fault: none of this can be our business.

Mother, I beg of you.

I told him no: I never meant to cross the river.

I live in a house

I live in a house without gardens or paths or miracles. I live in a house which is protected from the knives of the street by snails, birds and incantations. I live in a house which shudders with the praise songs of passing cars filled with sunglasses and guns and sperm. I live in a house which lures dappled shade to its front rooms every morning while heat drools through the back but each afternoon the roles reverse. I live in a house which stays sane only because the sun can move. I live in a house whose neighbours are neon and perpetual complacency. I live in a house where every day I open the doors and windows a little wider to allow winds to blow in between its walls. I live in a house which crumbles brick by brick in response to the entreaties of spurned beggars and homeless children. I live in a house with foundations still brooding for the tonguestrokes of the sea. I live in a house that is slowly becoming my body.

He had to come in

There were too many mosquitoes by now around the outside lamp so he had to come in. Besides, despite the moon, evening mist had covered up the dance of tiny mirrors on the vlei, the stars were all rubbed out, and he had no excuse left. He had sat still on the balcony for so long through the chill biting to his bones, though, that a marsh owl had perched on a stump a stone's throw away and scrutinised him fixedly for quite a while. For some reason this had made him uncomfortable.

– *What are you doing?* she said to him, as he closed the door. She was pretending to fuss over supper.

– *Nothing*, he said.

He glanced at her, tried to avoid scratching the open sores near his wrist until she stopped watching. She seemed really calm tonight.

– *You look a little less pale. Are you feeling ok?*

– *Well, at least I'm not losing weight any more*, he said.

– *Are you sure? You know the doctor said your cell count wasn't as it should be.* She picked up some knives and forks; dropped one. *And you still look so thin to me. Don't you think you should eat something? Don't you think …*

– *actually, I feel goddamn awful: are you happy that I've said it?* As soon as the words came out, he regretted them: she had decided not to leave him, after all.

– *I don't really know why you think you can still talk that way to me*, she said. She turned back to the counter and pretended to wipe it. He could see that she was going to start crying again, and sighed.

But she didn't. Instead, she turned fully to confront him: looked straight at him.

– *It's not* my *love that's killing you*, she said.

To be inside

In the forests of your hair
a white bird nests

its five fingers
                        I
no longer recognise

as my right hand.
Your jersey squeaks

and sobs as you remove
it, stippling skin

chafed in patterns. Under
your uplifted arms

linger two smudges
like a memory of smoke.

        *

On our first night
you bent down

to nuzzle my neck.
Your knees cracked. Your

nakedness glimmered forth
from a ruction of sheets

sucking light to you
a dark star. And lifted,

settled your body, with
care, to surround

me. Soft caress
of hands, piqued blood

of thighs. You spoke,
three athwart words

in an undisclosed
tongue – yet

will take flight
before I can awake,

leaving buttons
on my carpet

like the helmets
of mutineering soldiers.

INGRID DE KOK

Married late

I married early, then I married late.
Exchanged young folly for an older fate.
I swooped into marriage that first day
To find it was a landlocked place.
I married early, then I married late.

I wandered through the new estate.
The trees were tall, the walls were high.
I wanted to be kind and true
But then I saw an open gate.
I married early, then I married late.

I tried to close the gate.
I tried. It's no one's fault
I recognised the wild inside
And was found wanting.
I married early, then I married late.

The bush beyond the gate was cold.
Life was tangled, lovers cruel.
I held my hand before my face
To read my mind. I had to wait.
I married early, then I married late.

When wildness turned to clarity
I found a love; he found me.
The risks were bigger: age and death.
Great losses in each small embrace.
I married early, then I married late.

I married early, then I married late.
Exchanged young folly for an older fate.
My spotted hands reflect the sun.
I stretch my ageing limbs. I sing.
I married early, then I married late.

Stay here

For TM

Stay here, a little longer.
Stay here with me.

How easy it is for you to go,
step by step, print by print
as if you are just fetching
the washing off the line,
or stopping for the shopping
on your way from work,
just posting a subscription
for another year.

But ending up on another coast
where your dead are visiting overnight,
especially your wild friend
who wants your company so badly
he lies through his teeth,
promises if you stay night long,

there'll be wine, tobacco, debate,
and no women to call you back

importunately like this:
stay here a little longer, with me.

My muse is a man

My muse is a man, not a woman.
He corrects my first draft, and my second.
Not an icon, lure or projection,
no Dorothy, Beatrice, or Julia,
he's a critic, a judge and grammarian.
He demands accuracy as well as passion,
abhors emotion on the loose,
"imagination" as excuse.
Glowers over spacing and spelling.

While most muses are cryptic,
wild, mild or remote,
(or so I am told),
my muse has strong views.
He asserts the primacy of sound,
the way language must sing
in and for its cage of meaning.
Is scornful of lower case,
the elongated line,
the sentimental rhyme,
generic trees and birds,
harsh images of fathers.

He recites the words
of his real beloved
aloud and alone
though I eavesdrop in the shadows:
"Stand whoso list upon the slipper top."
Remembers everything he has read.
Believes the best poems speak of death.
Also love, but mostly death.
That's why my muse is a man.

Meeting after much time has passed

How are you he asked
And was I fine was I
I was
I said I was

Meetings between old lovers haters
Have a way of going along like this
Ja-nee
Yes fine

Hypodermic needle point
That's what it was like
With us before
But he looked well

And he said he was well
And I was fine yes
(Older fatter
But kinder better) very well too

Histoplasmosis: a guide's instructions at the cave

If after a few weeks you find yourself coughing,
your chest laced in a corset of steel,
tell your doctor you were here.
Tell him about the bats, their investment in the dark,
their droppings spongy fudge
which you probably tramped on in the cave,
the spores you may have breathed
now inhabiting your lung tissue,
taking all your breath
for the growing fungus
inside you.

Don't panic. There is medication for this
if you reach an informed doctor early enough.
Your airways can be cleared again,
lungs restored to normal size.
But remember, a bat flew into your body
out of a cave. Your body is now a cave.
Your breath is the way in and out of the cave,
its dark entrance the same as
its only exit.

Notes for that week

After Seferis

Friday
The sun throws its net
of peremptory shadows.
Across the road
noisy renovations,
then removal of rubble.

The doctor says the graph
is a source for concern.
He doesn't know
your arrhythmic heart
is playing a jazz theme.

Saturday
Remember, inaugural day
nineteen ninety-four,
our table piled with the future?
From the window we watched
three men in the street
search our garbage bin
for bread or bottles,
liberation's left-overs.

Sunday
I never get lost in the city streets
because I follow the same route,
park in the same lot,
visit the same bookshop

eat outdoors
have a cell phone ready.

There are some changes:
a building implodes,
on the foreshore a new one
aspires to interpret the century.
Men from the Congo
their eyes border-crossing,
safeguard the cars
in courteous French.
There are more children
though some are taller,
grow older, as we do.

Monday
On the corner a man
sells mobiles of yachts, cheap string

fraying in the hot wind.
His dog hardly stirs; nobody buys.

Tuesday
Women who live alone are precise.
In the laboratory of feeling
a pantry, preserves arranged
according to colour, date, size.
Kumquat, green fig, apricots in brandy.

Wednesday
The south-easter blows.
Wednesday's child is full of woe.

Thursday
Inside.
The house with the cool rooms in summer.
High ceilings, white mouldings.
Light filters through wooden blinds
onto books, sharpened pencils,
an unpolished desk, a silent telephone.
Who is sleeping away the long afternoon?

Outside.
The washing line shrouded by sheets
in the concrete courtyard.
Green mosaic of mint, sage and beans
and cheap red jewels: tomatoes, zagreb chillies.
The lime tree and its lightbulbs.
Frangipani dropping
unseasonal yellow and white tears
onto unmown grass.
The nuzzle of the sea breeze
in the greying fur of the cat.

What kind of man?

Tony Yengeni: "What kind of man are you? ...I am talking
about the man behind the wet bag."
Captain Jeffrey T Benzien: "...I ask myself the same question."
– Cape Town Amnesty hearings

I

It's the question we come back to.
After the political explanations
and the filmy flicker of gulags, concentration,
re-education and ethnic cleansing camps,
prisons and killings in the townships and fields,
here at the commission we ask again,
can't get away from it, leave it alone:
"What kind of man are you?"

II

What kind of man mounts another
in deadly erotic mimicry,
then puts a wet bag over his head
to suffocate him for "the truth"?

Lets her baby cry for her
from a nearby cell,
threatens to stop the crying?

Roasts meat on coals
while a man is burning on a nearby pyre?

Gives evidence like this
in daylight; but can give no account?

III

What kind of man are you?
What type? We ask and he asks too
like Victorians at a seminar.
Is it in the script, the shape of the head,
the family gene?
Graphology, phrenology or the devil?

IV

Nothing left but to screen his body.
We have no other measure
but body as lie detector,
truth serum, weathervane.

V

We look at his misshapen cheek,
how it turns away from questioning,
as if he's an abused child;

at his mouth, its elastic pantomime;

at his sagging chin, glottal Adam's apple,
throat no longer crisp from a morning razor;

at his eyes' pouches, pitted olives, dunes;

at the eyes themselves,
how they sweat, don't weep;

his ears, peaks on a listening uniform;

the hand with its thumb intact, its active fingers;

and the apparently depressed, possibly sedated,
shuffling lumbering cumbersome body
which then helpfully and earnestly
performs in slow motion with perfect memory
its training, its function: a tantric posture with wet bag
that just for a moment is so unbelievable
it looks like a pillow fight between brothers.

VI

Though of the heart we cannot speak
encased in its grille of gristle

the body almost but does not explain
"What kind of man are you?"

VII

This kind, we will possibly answer,
(pointing straight, sideways,
upwards, down, inside out):
this kind.

ROSAMUND STANFORD

Forefathers

Through the neck. On the back
of the back. Bent, bullied, boasted.
Stood. Slept against coir: its lumps.
Bones have stood vertical and held.
Held up. Tall. Hard. Bridges. To the
top of the day. The days. Every day.
Up. Upright. Arrow-browed. Gaunt
bridges: up of the plunging up.
Shouldering bones. Shouldering trees.
Shouldering progeny, storm-sodden
ewes. Raising. Lofted sheds. Planted
poles going high. Roofs lifting to a
pitch. Crops tall as cane. Thatch
streaked by season. Straight and dry.
Trees slowly. All over. Eucalypts. White
shanks into the cloud. Clouds on stalks.
Blood. Litmus of rising days. Sapgreen
insect juices into the up. Up. Standing.
Long cheekbones. Lean. Sculpts. Tall.
Tall hands. Nostril bones. Tall and
aquiline. Foreheads: Forefathers.
Coursing. Coursing. Bone.

Our president

Watch the soil mister president
watch it slide as you dance
See the stones slither in unison
as our nation takes on the
hooded manner of a rinkhals
a snake across Africa
At night the stones shiver into
a cowering semi-stillness
We are distressed and complicit
leader of the nation
Don't you want to tell us of our
forays in foreign lands
and of our land allotment plans?
We are nudging one another
watching as you dance
swaying and mesmerized
in a pall of smouldering questions
But we are vigorous
and don't mind a touch of the serpent
After all, who are we to exclude
when it was us, our very selves
put paid to exclusion
We are includers one and all
So we accept your serpent self
Let us use all our hands
to shake the restless land
back into a new stillness
to track the streamings
from your two-pronged tongue
Our valleys are slithering
in anticipation

Ditch

So I tried, tried living in a ditch
couldn't hear the acoustics down there
and the smell was grainy.
My drums loosened a bit, got softer and quiet,
I was quiet and quietened, talkless, and when I talked
it came out loud, words strode forth.
No I thought, turn them round, bend them over
put them back, cocoon them.

I kept some fat between my bones and my skin,
for cushioning purposes.
It was a good thing, I could lie quite still
and the cold came, but only slowly,
and quite quietly.
At first I'd felt warm,
warm as another person's warm shirt
warm as a streaming blonde day
Then the sun dropped over the edge,
risen out of my ditch, moved on.

That's okay I said, okay for it to vanish.
But I was not convinced.
It was propaganda of the kind kind,
the sort that mothers and their soothy ilk
had bathed me in:
No such thing as gloom, not in our life,
our life is very merry.

I lay there thinking of my formerly tight mouths
and cleanliness and warmliness and Stuttafords bra section
and my two breasts and how my shoulders cowed
forward to shelter them.

In the ditch my breasts were fine,
round and braless, they were lying quiet, silently and lazily,
one atop my chest, the other bulging a bit
over the edge of me.

They didn't mind anymore, of which I was glad.
They were comfortable for a change
even though it was extremely uncomfortable were I was.
In fact I would have liked a mattress,
but mattresses spring out of their seams in ditches,
show their skeletons. In any case
it's illogical to think you can have a mattress in a ditch
and I had logic on my side.

I had enough unseemly fat to cushion the earth
which, as I soon found out, was quite grateful
for the consideration I was showing it.
It: I thought. Is that alright:
a right way to think of the earth?
But what else is there: I've never been
one to think of the earth as a she
or cars either, and specially not ships (maiden voyages),
there's something obscene in calling a vessel she
(or the other way round).

It was uncomfortable as the night bore on
Not that I'd been expecting sleep,
I was awaiting and awaking, but parts of me
my eyes for example, were adroop,
I was like a hen or a horse, standing and sleeping
(although I wasn't sleeping and neither was I standing,
but I could just as well have been
for all the comfort of lying on that lumpen earth).
I didn't wish to be rude to the earth,

either the bits of it that I was lying on
or the whole thing
I was less comfortable than even those people
who used a stool-like carved thing for a pillow,
(rows and rows of them are on display in Museum Afrika).
Maybe they were better than a rock,
and good at stopping insects crawling into your earhole
and for keeping the earth-sound out.

I could hear the earth,
it was embarrassing, it was breathing,
but not in a relaxed continental way, not easy earthbreath.
It was breathing as if it knew someone had
their ear right on it, it couldn't completely let go.
If the sun had been shining it probably wouldn't have
minded my ear following each in and each out,
but at night with everything so quietened
the earth didn't feel free.
I began to feel intrusive: "I'll not hear" I said,
and for a while the earth breathing did ease a bit,
began to sound like the far-off swishing sea
but soon enough it realised that my ear was actually
not blockable, that my breathing was the breathing
of pretending to not listen, or not to hear,
that I couldn't not hear. So I gave up
and both of us, me and the earth, softened a bit.

Rustum Kozain

Kingdom of rain

from these I am growing no nearer
to what secret eluded the children
– Derek Walcott, "Sainte Lucie"

Somewhere in some dark decade
stands my father without work,
unknown to me and my brother
deep in the Paarl winter and a school holiday.
As the temperature drops, he,
my father, fixes a thermos of coffee,
buys some meat pies and we chug
up Du Toit's Kloof Pass in his old 57 Ford,
where he wills the mountain – under cold cloud,
tan and blue rock face bright and wet with rain –
he wills these to open and let his children in,
even as he apologises –
my strict and angry fearsome father –
even as he apologises for his existence
then and there his whereabouts declared
to the warden or ranger in government
issue, ever-present around the next turn
or lazing in a jeep in the next lay-by:
"No sir, just driving. Yes, sir, my car."

At the highest point of the pass
we stop to eat, and he, my father,
this strict and angry, fearsome father,
my father whom I love and his dark face,

155

he pries open a universe that strangely
he makes ours, that is no longer mine:
a wily old grey baboon, well hid
against salt-and-pepper rock, eyeing us;
some impossibly magnificent bird of prey
rarely seen, racing to its nest as the weather turns.
And we are up there close I think
to my father's God, the wind howling
and cloud rushing over us, awed
and small in that big car swaying in the gale.

Silence. A sudden still point
as the universe pauses, inhales
and gathers its grace.
Then the silent, feather-like fall
of snowflakes as to us it grants
a brief bright kingdom
unseen by the ranger. And for some minutes
a car with three stunned occupants
rests on a mountain top outside the fast
ever-darkening turn of our growing up;
too brief to light the dark years
when I would learn:

how the bright, clear haunts of crab and trout
where we swim in summer
now in winter a brown rage over rock;
how mountain and pine and fynbos
or the mouse-drawn falcon of my veld;
the one last, mustard-dry koekemakranka
of summer that my father tosses through the air
to hit the ground and puff like a smoke bomb;
and once, also in summer somewhere,
a loquacious piet-my-vrou;

or the miraculous whirligig of waterhondjies
streaking across a tea-coloured pool
cradled by tan rock and fern-green fern;
my first and only owl,
large and mysterious
in a deep stand of pine,
big owl we never knew were there
until you swooped away, stirred by our voices;
how I too would be woken and learn
that this tree and bird, this world
the earth and this child's home
already fell beyond his possessives.

And how, once north through the dry
Bushmanland with its black rock,
over a rise in the road, the sudden green
like the strange and familiar sibilants
in Keimoes and Kakamas.
And the rush of the guttural was the water
over rock at Augrabies.
The Garieb over rock at Augrabies,
at Augrabies where the boom swings down,
the gate-watch tight-lipped as a sermon:
"Die Kleurlingkant is vol"
as he waves through a car filled
with bronzed impatient white youth
laughing at us, at my father, my father
my silent father in whom a gaze grows distant
and the child who learns this pain past metaphor.
How like a baboon law and state
just turned its fuck-you arse on us
and ambled off.

Memory I

Comes through the bright green leaves
of the row of oak trees
in late November,

the whitewashed wall of the school.

The matric exam done,
we've come to return our textbooks
and now stand in the shade

under the big oak by the school hall
to say farewell
to a favourite teacher

who looks on us
with the care some always had,
our teachers,

but that we recognise
always only too late,
in memory

when we're looking elsewhere
for something else, like now,

when I look elsewhere,
for something else,
you come to me unbidden

under that tree,

Mnemosyne

in a short white dress
with small red flowers
or are they strawberries?

Your bare brown arms,
your athlete's calves
firm in tan sandal-straps,

your eyes also brown,
your hair, brown;

nut-brown hair
that will brush across my face
and all the stories before

and after, of how it begins
or ends
its tracery

fine as the veins on a bright green leaf
in a Boland summer
before we turn to the world:

you to study music
me to fail mathematics and turn
to the algorithms of heartbreak

and study its poetry instead,
its failed theorems
which, when one looks, lead back

to this sylvan scene
where you were the first woman I loved.
Though still I don't know what it means,

I loved you deeply,
in all its infinite innocence,
deep enough

it hurt me into poetry
like a country would
like a country does;

into the poetry
that brings me back
to the barbs and pull of memory.

*

Who cares now
that these lines are sentimental,
when it's not done

to sing of love in youth
to apostrophise
some big Romantic Absence

to be instead self-aware
of the sin of emotion.

But here they are,
lines I wish I could have written
when I was another,

lines other
than those cribbed
from pop songs and embroidered hangings,

before I studied heartbreak.

*

It's no more done
that men should cry thus in public
or anyone

should talk of hurt
unfixed by chemicals
or by money to buy things.

But here it is:

That cut below the heart,
the one that never heals
the one we won't admit

for fear of seeming weak
but also
to guard its privacy,

the hurt we wish forgotten,
that hurt lasts
and lasts as long

as a word like "slave" survives.

Look at us,
still hurt
here

or into a scatter of lone rituals
buying up redemption
in malls across the world.

A public hurt, Apartheid hurt us
somewhere outside history
beyond statistics

or the careful prose of glossed reports;
hurt us
beyond the weal of reparations,

a pittance from some pig-fat,
over-lording bureaucrat
or the cheap spectacles of sport and reconciliation.

It hurt us where it only multiplies
I now declare
in the private heart

because our hurt is still our sin

and wished forgotten
like a date of battle
or some other minor detail

ill-chosen,
a part of speech
beyond our parsing.

And so we carry on, hurting.

Leaving

You brought me mangoes, overripe
with a fizz in their yellow flesh:
the tang of home-made ginger beer –
my childhood – you took from your bag,
opening your palms to sunset.

*

The day breaks. We move into
each other, huddle in every known
hollow, and make love one more time.
Then we drink the last of the wine,
our favourite, for breakfast ...

Afterwards, I look at your blood
pearling small berries in my hair
drying on my thigh in patches
darker than my skin: like wine
this blood that numbs the cut
of our parting.

That river, that river

For Sean Africa

Then there's one moment I'm doing everything:
dusting books, shelving them.
Brewing coffee.
On the stereo

Bob Marley, slow and sad:
"Johnny was a good man,
never did a thing wrong."
Another moment

and Melancholia is my name.
And I'm floating down a river,
down that river,
down that river,

sifting through a pile of chapbooks,
then regret, regret.
I tell you, Regret is my name.
And Desolate my heart's.

A funeral programme,
the photograph of an old friend,
his hint of a jowl
like mine too now in age.

I look for him now
down that river, that river,
paging the thin programme:
the pallbearers' names ring in long friendship

from home, into the church,
out of the church;
names who are still here to bear you
and me through the estranging decades.

But then there are only pages of hymns,
thin, inconsequential hymns
in the new, awkward poetry, or no poetry:
"Yea, though I walk through death's dark vale."

What kind of God will respond
to His own absence in the mirror we hold to Him?
When God Himself is inconsequential?
As this funeral programme now is

with its inconsequential notes
scribbled in my own inconsequential hand:
"Thunder rolling over the Boland"
and whispers overheard from schoolchildren,

or, no, it was from a friend: *"Juffrou is ook hier."*

Juffrou is ook hier. Five syllables
and a life of consequence,
full of chalkboards and class registers,
the dedicated *Juffrou* who worries

about the children, all the children,
and the slowest among them,
whether they've eaten, whether there's trouble
at home and in your heart again.

Juffrou is ook hier.

In that moment comes a life
more full than any poetry
or the prose of the anthropologist;
a poetry of consequence more than any god's ken

and which is solace to all my names,
a raft down that river,
that river, that river.
Who knows how strong that river,

Sean,
that river that took you in?
Meneer Africa, of solace
and consequence

to the schoolchildren
who knew your care
and who now stand by the river,
thunder rolling in over the Boland,

rain over the warm earth
and up in the mountains
more water over rock,
more rivers gathering strength.

Dear Comrades

You who once were children, students,
young athletes become the heroes
of we the people warmly teeming
in the joyful new republic of your dreams,
a fulsome, healthy common weal;
you who once yourselves were dreaming heroes
in your speechifying or in striking poses
defiant and heroic like Olympic gods
with raised fists over balustrades,
from balconies and stages
overlooking us,
and at the sides of graves
in vigil overlooking fallen comrades
believing their blood makes fruitful
the earth of what would be that new republic.

A NEW republic!
How daring you were then,
almost almost the gods
we were keening for, that we had made.
How daring then to have just that:
a dream. Just a dream.
Yet how *you* dreamed. In your dream
you were become a god who could defy the force of death.

And we would harbour you,
we the people in our council houses,
our shacks in winter damp –
was where we harboured you.

There we shared our consolations
with wood smoke from the coal stove

or the smell of paraffin.
There we cut the meat
into smaller, meagre pieces
made more to share with you;
added half a cup more meal
so you too could eat, then sleep and dream
that dream which we too dreamed,
that dream in which we came upright
fully human, warm and dry.

That dream that was so fierce.

Did you then *believe* that dream?
Or back then dreamt already
of a house of proper, bourgeois dream
somewhere overlooking the sea
from where you would no longer
have to worry about still *over*looking us;
dreamt already then
of how you'd sell our foolish dream,
or rip it
into the gilded tatters
of your newfound love for dear commodities –
a new, expensive car,
whiskies and cigars,
the fine cloth of another land –
the contraband you trade in off our useful dream.

We are now become your fools,
our heroes' fools.
Jeered at
for having believed in dream,
for having not known
that our better future

was forever always lost,
then already would have held the bitter dregs
and our heroes, you, always then already bound
in any case to end up
loosening forever the belt around your widening girth.

We admit, declare,
declare that we were fools to dream beyond our brokenness,
and that now breaks us more.
We must admit
we're broken,
but broken from your dream.

Comrade, you must know
that dream we dreamed is dead,
that dream in which you once were almost god
is no longer yours. You can muster
only soporifics
like a wizened walrus lolling in the sun
or like your children too, fattening
like grubs on the food chain of this fetid ecology,
the corpse of our dream-dead republic.

You must know
you are no more a thing of us,
of our creation,
no more the welcome guest
when once again we build a dream.

Death

Father, five vodkas and I hear
death coming: the rustle of leaves
in the yard; the bougainvillaea

that scratches at the roof
like the six-year-old street kid
who tugs at my shirt sleeve.

The vast insides of my country
that coil around its ulcer and its ache.
These stars could console

but not tonight. Between me and them
there's just the cold wind sniping,
just the vast black night.

Stars of stone

Today the stones I know will nick
our skulls, then knock our souls
from us. It is so. For under stars
that are but burning stone,
we held each other. Named for light,
Nurbibi clung to me, her back
against the flat roof of my house
warding off earth, hanging
under heaven. Face-down,
I gripped her shoulders, smelled
the stone roof through the rug.
Nurbibi may have stared
over my shoulder at the stars,
those burning bits of far-off stone.

And she may have seen four men's eyes
hanging above us in their own,
unmoving flame. Eyes of stone,
heads shrouded in swathes
of scripture. So I, Turyalai,
am bound. And on my knees.
And Nurbibi, in whose loins I sought
some God, is now almost at one
with earth, buried to her waist
next to me. We wait
for the seekers of God
and their ceremony of the stone.
Men we do not know will come
and let stone speak, first in whispers

then in what they must believe
a chattering of angels

171

when the crowd erupts and rocks arc
but in parabolas far short
of reaching God, that must return
to earth. Men who do not know us.
Men who cannot know
that even as we wronged my wife,
in union we created God. In come-cries
caught in the throat, we made Him.
And made Him ours, gave Him some voice
even as He was in the still of night
as He is now, inchoate
before the hard and burning stars.

*Turyalai and Nurbibi were accused of adultery and
stoned to death by the Taliban in November 1996.*

172

GABEBA BADEROON

Fit

Dim light of the tailor shop, small bell calling
him from the back, shelves with their bottles
of buttons, a thimble, dust and thread
of cuttings on the floor.

To make a coat, search
in all the fabric shops from Wynberg
to Town for cotton, linen, wool.

He licks a forefinger to turn a new page
in the small black book with red binding
and, holding a thick stub of pencil, measures
the arm from collarbone to wrist, elbow bent.

At the waist, two fingers go
on the inside of the measuring tape
to allow a give of flesh between
the measure and the fit.

He translates the length and hardness
of the bones, the breath and change
of the human body
into the flat numbers of the pattern.

*

My father, a tailor, loved to see
my mother wear the clothes he made for her.

173

At the fitting, holding pins at the side
of his mouth, he lifts the dress from its hanger,
seams pressed but not yet finished
with buttons and hem.

She puts it on, turning
the cloth from two dimensions into three.
Always this taking shape around the body,
this translation again of the breath into the fit.

To watch my mother's coat as she hurried
out of the house on her way to work, the swish
of her dress in the slipstream of her walk,
was to discover a rhythm too fine to see
in the steps themselves. To grasp it fully,
you had to watch her clothing as she left.

I forget to look

The photograph of my mother at her desk in the fifties
has been in my purse for twenty years,
its paper faded, browning,
the scalloped edge bent then straightened.

The collar of her dress folds discreetly.
The angle of her neck looks as though
someone has called her from far away.

She was the first in her family to take
the bus from Claremont
up the hill to the university.

At one point during the lectures at medical school,
black students had to pack their notes, get up and walk
past the ascending rows of desks out of the theatre.

Behind the closed door, in an autopsy
black students were not meant to see,
the uncovering and cutting of white skin.

Under the knife, the skin,
the mystery of sameness.

In a world that defined how black and white
could look at each other, touch each other,
my mother looks back, her poise unmarred.

Every time I open my purse,
she is there, so familiar I forget
to look at her.

The pen

Three days before my father died
I lost the silver pen with my name on it,
a twenty-first birthday gift from my aunt
I'd kept for almost ten years.

That day, supervising students in Khayelitsha
putting up a netball hoop, I came home
to ask to borrow his tools.
We walked round the garage and I ticked
off the ladder, drill, nails and screwdriver on my list,

and he suggested I add a hammer and level.
Somewhere between stacking and loading
the car, I lost my pen without even noticing
it had slipped from my hand.

When I went home late that day,
I negotiated with loss as I always do,
not going back to the garage to look for the pen
in case it wasn't there,
to keep its absence incomplete
so it could come back one day.

In three days
the impossible sequence of death.

I went back
over everything we'd said that day
and the years when we didn't speak
and the reconciliation, almost wordless,
when we walked towards each other with our eyes down
and wept while we hugged.

The night he died
I felt the completeness of loss,
of absence without negotiation,

and yet what was still there,
that moving towards each other,
without looking.

Postscript

In my old bedroom I reach for boxes
and the dust of undisturbed years rises
in the afternoon light. As children we drew

our names on such powdered floors. I flick
through high school report cards, forgotten
library books, letters now tearing and flaking.

My hand pauses on an envelope, sealed but unsent.
On the front, the name of our neighbours,
on the back, above the name of my family, I slide
a finger under the flap and tear open the years.
Inside, I find, on a Christmas card two decades old,
a greeting to the tailor next door, who has since died,
in the writing of my father, who has since died.

How brief and irretrievable our actions,
the writing and the forgetting,
and the lives that unfold from them.
Opening a letter not addressed to me,
I wonder if I am stealing a gift,
or completing a small, necessary ritual.

In the dusty room I say their names out loud
and place the card again among the old papers.

True

To judge if a line is true,
banish the error of parallax.
Bring your eye as close as you can
to the line itself and follow it.

A master tiler taught me this.

People wish to walk where he has kneeled
and smoothed the surface.
They follow a line to its end
and smile at its sweet geometry,
how he has sutured the angles of the room.

He transports his tools by bicycle –
a bucket, a long plastic tube he fills with water
to find a level mark, a cushion on which to kneel,
a fine cotton cloth to wipe from the tiles the dust
that colours his lashes at the end of the day.

He knows how porcelain, terracotta and marble hold
the eye. He knows the effect of the weight
of a foot on ceramic. Terracotta's warm dust cups
your foot like leather. Porcelain will appear
untouched all its life and for this reason
is also used in the mouth.

To draw a true line on which to lay a tile,
hold a chalked string fixed
at one end of a room and whip
it hard against the cement floor.

With a blue grid, he shakes out
the sheets of unordered space, folds
them into squares and lays them end on end.
Under his knees, a room will become whole and clear.

At night, he rides home over ground that rises
and falls as it never does under his hands.

Where nothing was

When we met and your face first
clarified itself
from the world,

I tried to find a word
to show where in the chest
two senses fired

at once,
muscle and hum,
a word for touch and sound together.

Like the thrum when
the metal chain of an anchor
whips hard and holds.

Or the clout of hands
as trapeze artists grasp each other,
the brief, final clasp

of coming to rest
where you knew
nothing was

a moment before.

Cinnamon

I fall outside
the warm stole
of history.

Eyes run down my skin
like a single finger.

I find you

open as a tent.
You are cinnamon
curved around me.

DENIS HIRSON

Scar

The young man sat in his mother's flat, sawing at a cello
with his long arms, over and over, the notes accumulating
like branches of wood, and his bearded El Greco face
bent to the music that continuously escaped him.
It was a late winter's afternoon in Johannesburg, and the sun
hung soft and ripe above the rocks of Linksfield Ridge
when finally the cello was laid down and the man
went out, walking the slopes with his girlfriend and me,
the anxious strokes of music still hatching the stiff cold air
all around us. I cannot say how it happened
but suddenly two dogs were fighting, almost at my feet,
rasping and savagely barking as if all the murder hidden
in the underside of the city had struck a sound in their throats.
Without thinking, I wedged a hand between them
and had it bitten to the bone. The white scar
still points down to the hollow of my palm, reminding me
of my mother's fierce glance upon the wound and my stupidity,
the voice of the cellist's girlfriend singing in my ear:
How your mother gives herself to her anger!
All of this written in my right hand: the broken music
and the vengeful land, my mother and her merciless giving.

Initiation

In the Bois de Vincennes, mighty chestnut trees
raise the white wick of their blossom,
tier upon tier into the late May sky

while down below, their trunks become goal-posts
for a dusty, milling host of boys.
A few paces away,

in the chestnuts' wide and pleasant shade,
my son stands at a park-bench, wipes an eye
and raises his forearm, displaying to an older friend

his first true, red-glazed gash, gained after skidding
into a tackle. The friend gives it a glance,
then rolls a trouser-leg to the knee,

displaying his own pedigree of welt and scar,
truth notched in their skin for all to see:
no wounds, no history.

Time lines

I remember my mother rushing out of the door in her white coat in the morning and my father leaving for a walk after dinner and not coming back. I remember how much time there was at night with no parents and a bored maid gazing at a wall in the kitchen. I remember when the bird in my dark chocolate cuckoo clock got stuck and let out a dry squawk. I remember lying in bed tracing a figure-eight with my big toe against the upper sheet, and thinking about something I seemed to have thought about before but that dissolved as I lay there thinking about it. I remember my father calling out "Durban time" in a low sing-song voice to wake me up in the half-light so we could all go on holiday. I remember "What's the time?" "Time you got a watch"; "What's the time? Half past my freckle", and "What's the time? Half past nine, Hang your broekies on the line". I remember learning that in the time it takes to say "one hippopotamus" slowly, a second has gone by. I remember watches with a thin red second hand; watches that told you on the back how many jewels there were inside, and waterproof watches that weren't. I remember watches with a little window for the day and another one for the date that was always wrong. I remember our teacher asking us how long we thought our bones would last. I remember "The worms crawl in, the worms crawl out, They crawl in thin and they crawl out stout, Awoo ahee, awoo ahee, ahappy we will be". I remember when we went to a funfair and the

183

Zulu watchman came up and told us everything was closed because Strydom had just died. I remember an Afrikaans song on the radio with an accordion and a man singing all the months of the year in a jovial voice that sounded as if he had just had a lot of beer and a braai. I remember the four o'clocks growing among the blackjacks near our back fence. I remember discovering what "five o'clock shadow" meant and looking at men to see if they had any on their faces. I remember the problem of finding a man who would teach me how to shave. I remember prefects on gate duty, and late detention. I remember the teacher who used to tell us we would be late for our own funeral. I remember 90 day detention, and 180 day detention. I remember when people were reading Arthur Koestler's *Darkness at Noon*. I remember the "Sunrise, sunset" song in *Fiddler on the Roof*, with the line "Is this the little girl I once knew?" I remember my mother telling me how she was on her way home from medical school and I came rushing up the road to meet her. I remember listening to Bob Dylan singing "Time passes slowly when you're searching for love", and wondering why, if he was right, time seemed to be passing so quickly for me. I remember The Byrds singing "To everything, turn, turn, turn, There is a season, turn, turn, turn, And a time for every purpose under heaven." I remember Donald Campbell and his Bluebird, Paul Nash with his smooth brown hair, licking everyone in the world at 100 yards until something went wrong with his bones, and Stirling Moss who had such an unlikely surname for a racing driver. I remember when I was about to fall in love for the first time, and the girl in question was wearing trousers, sitting cross-legged under a table and talking to a girlfriend at a party in someone's Johannesburg flat. I remember that when I met the woman I was going to marry, the first thing we talked about was our grandmothers. I remember the sound of our daughter's heart, audible thanks to a monitor in the delivery room before she was born, like a horse that was softly pounding with great speed towards us.

Cider and water

For Adine

The man sold the best cider in the country
in an old stone house at the edge of the woods.
He had sloping fields of apple trees
with a few grey donkeys beneath them,
baring their teeth as they lifted their necks
to reach for the fruit hanging red among the leaves.

Come into my arms, and tell me what love is.

Why did he need to speak to us so badly?
Why insist that we meet the new woman in his life?
There she was, standing out on the grass
in the sweet mellow sunlight of late August,
in a dress that was too short, and too blue,
wearing cracked nail polish and a humble smile.

Come into my arms,
I want to smooth your forehead,
sink my face against your face
and let its beauty cover me like water.

I was slightly drunk after trying all his drinks,
some rough as sandpaper, some light and airy.
He sold mead too, with a taste of potent apple juice
that had swallowed dark hives of honey.
Behind him: plump wooden casks in an ancient cellar.
Before him: the new woman, fetched

from a country in north Africa many seek to flee.
She would lie down alongside his loneliness.
He would give her half his bed, stamping her passport
with the stiff flesh of his want.
Still, he would not allow her to have a child,
he was too old for that now, his children grown

while she was ripe for motherhood and a family of her own.
Where could she turn, lost even before she met him
in a country of men who would only marry a virgin;
a bought wife now, with eager face and broken French,
hands calloused from her cleaning job in a local hotel,
smiling quietly next to the man who had imported her life.

Come into my arms,
I want to hold your face that brought me
from the deep dry well where I turned
in circles around myself.
Love survives in the most unlikely places.
Let me sink my face against your face
and feel its beauty cover me like water.

Doctor fish

There are these fish.
You put your legs in the water
and they nibble off the scars.
You find them in Turkey and China
and Croatia. Have you ever felt a mouth
softer than moss, wetter than sex
eating at you, have you ever felt the shadow
of pain rolling off like a stocking ?
You find them in Belgium and South Korea
and Singapore. You put your heart in the water
and they nibble off the scars. Health authorities
have ruled this practice to be unsanitary.
They say tools need to be discarded or sanitized
after use. It doesn't help, they say,
to wash out the fish tank. But have you ever
felt the blow of loss dissolving like a biscuit
in your coffee? These fish have mouths
that will tickle you pink.
You find them in the Netherlands
and India and Greece. You
put your memory in the
water and they nibble
till it floats up
shivering like a
bubble.

The song of the crows

Crows find the human voice far too melodious,
too full of intonations and accents. Why go
to all that trouble if you've got one good long note

raw and rusty as a spade left out in the rain
that digs into the sky as you rise and fly,
any emotion from a sob to a gob of laughter

scrawled out through your windy beak and scattered
all around you for the other crows to pick up
and repeat? When you're a crow, originality

is no question, you hop along in the grass
like all the rest, wear your hair short,
hop some more, rustle your serrated wings

and sing your only crow song, thrusting it
over your black shoulder as you ride the currents,
love and death and memory crunched

and shoved into your crow voice with no time
for scales or inflection, only the bitter blunt
essentials, one sound plundered to perfection.

Why dogs would make good writers

They feel no guilt.
They go nose first
where hunger takes them.
They bite to the bone.

When they're done
they lie out in the grass,
paws crossed,
sticking out their tongues.

JOAN METELERKAMP

Points on poems

1. You can begin at any point.

2. You might be asked to account for yourself
   (you are always asking yourself to account for yourself);
   you could start with the point that poems don't sell
   take stock of that fact
   prevaricate, equivocate,

3. leave it as a starting point, for later, balance
   interest, currency, the market;

4. you could come back to it before you had begun you could cycle
   round lugubriously, alternatively

5. get on your bike and ride like hell like we used to, my brothers and
   I, when we were kids –
   careening round the concave concrete cow-shed yard –
   no brakes, no gears –
   sweaty and queasy and
   sometimes skidding on bull-shit.

6. Go, go with its elliptical spin, which is also weirdly comforting
   because

7. a poem has no point.

8. You could begin again: there is not one point to a poem
   it is always
   another point of departure.

9. Try another point of departure,
       say: poems are like music, not music, but like – the lines
          climax, silence, sound
          their own melodies, yes, but visions
          a score of complex
          moments in process emotion almost beyond words most of all
    what you can hardly, hardly, say, hardly, hardly bear to see, see and then

10. revision. Re-vision, if you must.

11. (Now you see it now you don't).

12. Okay, okay *no ideas but in things* the thing is

13. always the poem:

14. not a record –
    a resonance.

15. But at what point do I come in, you could say,
    and I could say
    either through your eye, through your ear,
    or – what my mother used to say (to thin air)
    when someone in another car hadn't thanked her for letting them in –

16. "not at all".
    Either you get it or you don't.

17. You could ask who speaks when the speaker is I.

18. The point is whose voice, out of the blue, into thin air,
    uses "I", like a child shrieking "me me me",
    or otherwise playing quietly outside under the pines
    whispering "you" "he" "she"?

19. Yours. Mine.

20. The point is: a poem is not a confession,
    it's not a profession (you could go back to the starting point)
    why you do it – it's a puzzle –

21. you could start at the edges
        or go for the gold in the middle –
        the bits where you can't tell
    the reflection from the craft
    floating on the surface, a coracle,
    and the more you piece together
    the figure – like the Lady of Shallot
    drifting through the reeds alone –
    the more she looks like your daughter
    or you, when you were younger,
    only where is the river running you begin to wonder
    and anyway
    there's always a bit missing
    and we all know it doesn't really help –
    the picture, on the box –

22. you're always figuring out
    what isn't fixed even if you think it is: or
    it is
    but still, and precisely still –

23. even though my brother, when we were older
    (though, according to the song, I'm so much younger than that
    now)
    and I was already a mother,
    used to say: don't fix it unless it's broken.

24. This is an old story

like Keats's figures on the jar,
still chasing
what they want, what they want to become,
happy, happy –

but everything empty, the vessel, the town –
they'll never be more than they are.

25. A poem is like
    live drawing the essential figure moving,
    how do you get it moving

26. across the page?
    (There should be no limit to the number of pages.)

27. It has nothing to do with linear narrative
    even though it's made of lines,
    and although it is really a story,

28. where to begin? What is the point
    of entry?

29. The song of the fertility doll (phallic and female)
    the energy that's divine
    (golden girl playing the piano
    easy, jazzy, smiling, explaining
    her hands are two Russian dolls
    they do exactly what she tells them to).

30. What on earth am I talking about – *cling, cohere, persevere?*

31. Don't ask unless you think it's somehow answerable or unavoidable,

32. like voices.

33. St Joan believed even when she couldn't hear the voices any longer

34. to the point of burning alive.

35. What do the voices say?
     What do you feel?
     Can you make them come

36. like someone else's voice? Another poet's?
     These poems are usually the best.
     As though someone else's words came into your head when you wake
     like after the recurring dream of intruders,
     you're sweating that fear of death sweat you've spent all this time
     worrying at that point you know
     Eliot made sixty years ago "the still point of the turning world"

37. and he was only re-writing the ancients and

38. who gives you the right to write what you like
     any way, who's to say if it makes any sense,
     any one – anyway –
     all poems are illegitimate.

39. Get used to this. You can't do anything else.
     Language itself is the transgressor.
     We know this. This is as old as Prometheus.
     "Yes, but what does this mean?"
     Nothing to do with what those who know better call
     "your personal life".

40. Who do you think you're talking to in that tone of voice
     like "get a life"?

41. You, me; myself – a poet is always talking to herself –

even more than to the dead. Answering back.

42. If the poem makes its own meaning, makes it up as it goes along,
    (I could come back to this) is something (what thing –
    the thing the poem is) prior to the poem –
    need the question arise?

43. It does
    arise
    like a god rises
    you can't not
    feel this
    through the slit through the curtains
    white light of the night
    turning to day
    like a lover turning over
    through that opening, that parting,
    that deep coming leaving
    only your need
    to speak –

44. Then instead of moving
    through the cool passages of an imagined labyrinth
    you get your head tangled, line after line
    like a spider in a spider's web:
    Arachne, still weaving the stuff out of herself,
    battered over the head with her own distaff
    by the jealous goddess;
    rather be Ariadne,
    lending her golden thread
    to her hero, to find his way out of the labyrinth,
    yes, he abandons her, but who finds her in the end:
    the one who comes back: Dionysus.

45. What labyrinth?
When the crystals are dislodged
the diamond body falls,
you feel as though you might fall over yourself
every time you reach upwards,
even if it's to hang out the washing.
If you think I'm talking about the inner ear I am.

46. If you are too sentimental or conventional for your crystals
ever to be knocked out of place
the poems you prefer will be sentimental and conventional –
probably in tight little rooms
(room = stanza, in Italian, no doubt someone will explain)
with a witty bit left hanging which could be anyone's
do not disturb sign
(you never know what's going on in there)
[of course there are little rooms where when
is a jar not a jar but a door left just off its jamb
opening something we didn't know we could imagine].

47. If you lose your balance completely no one will want to follow
there.

48. "Sixth and lastly" – as the dogsbody policeman says –
Much Ado about Nothing –
the main point about poetry

49. you don't find it in airports or bookclubs,
and if Nadine Gordimer were to ask you
if she could publish your work
for some cause, like AIDS, or even with no cause
with no payment to you at all you'd say, here, have it *all*,
please.

50. Cold comfort: the so-called
    helpers at the bookshop in Plettenberg Bay
    have never heard of Nadine Gordimer.
    So how do you make a living, poet, I ask myself,
    not for nothing

51. there are more ways of silencing a poet than with a Sentence.

52. This has nothing to do with The People's Poet.

53. This has nothing to do with The Woman Poet.

54. (The point is, nice girls always lie –
    to protect the innocent –
    there is a point beyond which
    they do not think;
    think what their good friends
    might think.)

55. If it's only amusement play, play,
    taking yourself seriously, amusing yourself, seriously,
    see what keeps
    coming up
    like say you keep coming up with an old symbol,
    the Dionysian heart in a basket,
    how do you say it –

56. the heart's thought, what does it mean, the eternal return,
    like the baby's heart on the monitor
    your own arrhythmia
    heart in your head on the bed –

    Not the apotheosis but the pattern the poet said.

57. But the pattern always appears
    when you're doing something else
    following some other thread
    you aren't listening or looking
    you're driving towards
    something else,
    like driving in the heat of the day up Keyter's Nek
    to fetch your teenage son after school
    head cruising any way
    into the road's rhythm, the heat,
    windows wide, words gone any way
    like *affirmation of the affirmation,*
    and you know this has very little to do with "positive thinking"
    in fact you're beginning to think it's the opposite,
    the words return, and there's no way to pull off the road,
    pull out of its rhythm to look, listen,
    to make them some pattern
    some sound to hear clearly not like like, like love, like love,
    not like this, this,
    but I've lost it again like this –
    not some thing   like love   not like   any thing   but this.

58. Or you wake in the night to the hot still after a storm,
    one of the two black south-eastern warning storms of the season,
    mud smell of water receding,
    frogs down below in the vlei,
    listen,
    an old propeller, an old engine, an old crock car,
    and you don't mind any more where you're spinning in any old
    world
    nor that the song the frogs make
    makes no more sense than this –
    the ballad the wind sings through the reeds
    through the house on a hot afternoon, sad,

repetitive, like to a baby in the bulrushes (the heart in a basket)
the scales you can hear clearly
of what the poet calls *marvellous*

out of sight out of mind
below surface,
(like a mole-rat shaking and shaking the roots of a khakibos
and all you can see is the thin plant shaking: okay, take it, it's just
a weed.)

59. Below surface, the words of the dead,
    dreams, too.
    I'll make one point: a poet can't live in daylight too long:
    the chainsaw in the valley;
    the chainsong of canaries, cisticolas, sombre bulbul, sunbirds,
    despite the cloud cover;
    the script of named fynbos; the clear horizon, the still sea;
    the discomfort of day's plans, narratives, narratives.

60. Wake to a snippet of dream recalled:
    I am off to get my own handcuffs, my own truncheon,
    hurry up they're waiting for me
    on the other side of the street like opposite the parking lot
    they blew up in Pretoria
    and I am young again as I was then when I lived in Pretoria.

61. Not what he *said* in the dream,
    what he *felt*, felt what I
    felt, I was dreaming, I felt his coming in,
    I think he said something,
    I felt I was coming in like through a door
    through my body
    I felt his cock I took it held it to my breathing
    I am alive so loudly I am grunting in, I am

aware even in the dream of my breathing
his speaking saying
take it
take it in.

62. I suppose I may have invented him; I may have been given him:
I didn't choose the metaphor, it chose me, came to me;
like a voice, like given words,
a message, open at this passage:
the activity of perception or sensation in Greek is aesthesis which
means at root "taking in" and "breathing in" – a "gasp", that primary
aesthetic response.

63. Only it didn't feel like a message, but a man.
Like a poem. Not like love but love.

64. There is only one point – begin again – make a poem of it –

See notes for "Points on poems" at the end of the anthology.

Intact

we are back
to back
you sink in
to sleep

I am lying as still as I can trying to still my sleeplessness
I feel the breathing wall of you that's why I married you I say

to die with
completely
contradictory
as always
as always
to live with
you say
though I thought you were asleep

I am the wind you are
the grass blown back the grass I am
the grass you are the wind blown back the wind

Deliver her from the depths
libera animas de profundo lacu

I stand in my new house, Mother,
first days of clear cold again
as if there could already be
          another winter, coming.

I stand in your green shoes
feet on thick soles,
wide enough
for your knitted socks,
          though this is already, another age

(come into my house, come in Mother,
knit socks if you like,
talk to me, tell me you are here,
help me with hems of cold curtains
where they drag across the bright floor)

see me, Mother, as I stand in your shoes, black river below me,

river of dreams, river of blood, bedded in earth

see me, in your grandson's room
as I slide aside his curtains,
new, which we chose, still a child,
still wanting to show you
see the curtains with their delicate
fishes and suns, green moons
and blue striated like the sea?
wide curtains, drawn aside, to take in,
momentarily, taking your breath, drawing closer, clearer,

river's outlet to the sea.

running all night, all night without us, without telling us,
was it always, was it years, stiller and stiller,
into the bed, into the bed rock –

*little words, little water-tight boat enough
funeral canoe, dug-out mokoro,
boat of words, take me to her:*

*steady paddles dipping,
procession of make-shift vessels,
paper boats, kissing the water,*

*river of black
stained with tannin of tree
iron of rock, salt of sea,
river of blood
waiting
for no-one, for nothing,
to the mouth
to the sea.*

ISOBEL DIXON

The skinning

I watched my older cousin skin a mole:
it seemed a fearsome thing to do, but I was eager
to be big and full of knowledge, so I stayed there,
brave girl, hunkered down, my flowered skirt
rucked up between my summer knees.
The shed's stone step – his rough autopsy table –
pressed the morning's gathered heat into my soles,
the same heat rising through the opened body
of the mole. I frowned against the boomerang
of sun, flung, swerving, off the blade at me,
and in the quiet of the early afternoon – the grown-ups
at their ritual naps – the whispering, *skrrt-skrrt*,
skin peeling back as if from velvet fruit, rasped
louder than the new, enormous thudding of my heart.

No bigger than a mango really, it had fitted in his palm
after the shot, a trophy for his patience, waiting, poised,
brave backyard hunter, ready finger on the trigger lip.
Unsuspecting, it had snuffled to the ceiling of the lawn,
a creature from a picture book, old Mouldiwarp: soft snout,
a pair of small, intrepid claws, a grubby engineer
whose only fault was choosing my aunt's emerald pride
and joy as his back door. But now it lay as dumb
as fruit, and leaking juice, a thick and sweethot scent
I had to suck my teeth against – but no, I wouldn't
look away, or pinch my nose, as his brown fingers,
almost priestly, probed the tight-packed inner things.

I watched, and didn't flinch: his certainty and skill –
and then his sudden, flashing grin, conspiratorial,
as though I wasn't just a scaredy-cat who couldn't catch
a ball or swim: I'd crouched to skin a mole with him,
and so I too, accomplice now, was in on his small kill.

Tear

The phone is a cruel mouthpiece,
pain's propaganda tool. A megaphone
for our confusion, for the rest
only delivering half.

My cheerful voice reverberates
until he thinks I've gone, the battery's dead,
and cuts the call. After the click
I let my choked throat spill,
go whimpering around the house,
folding up clothes.

The tickling on the inside of my thigh
becomes a wash of blood.
I stare with dumb eyes at the towel's stain –
it's not my time, my bleeding's past.
I must have wept my insides raw:
stigmata for my father
and his panel-beaten heart.

After grief

Three drops of lavender in this water
is not balm enough.
Red thyme, a pungent antiseptic,
will not purge this day.
But I shall have it, scent and life.
I will not bathe in only salt and blood.

Back in the benighted kingdom

I'm sorry to see
my mosquito bumps fade:
the love bites of a continent,
marks of its hot embrace.

If anything is dark,
it's this damp island
with its sluggish days,
its quieter, subtler ways
of drawing blood.

FINUALA DOWLING

At eighty-five, my mother's mind

When she wanders from room to room
looking for someone who isn't there,

when she asks where we keep the spoons,
when she can't chew and spits out her food,

when her last dim light flickers with falling ash
and she exclaims: "What a dismal end to a brilliant day!"

When she calls her regular laxative an astronaut,
When she can't hear words but fears sounds,

when she says: "Don't go – I can't bear it when you go,"
or: "Just run me off the cliff,"
or wants to know how many Disprin ends it,

then I think how, at eighty-five,
my mother's mind is a castle in ruin.

Time has raised her drawbridge, lopped her bastions.
Her balustrade is crumbled, and she leans.

Yet still you may walk these ramparts in awe.
Sometimes, when she speaks, the ghostly ensign flies.

Time cannot hide what once stood here
or its glory.

Do not think that we are good
or merely tourists.

That which detains us
was once our fortress.

Widowhood in the dementia ward

"Oh my God, I'm so pleased to see you,"
she says from her nest of blankets.
"I've been meaning to ask –
How is your father?
How is Paddy?"

"He died," I say, remembering 1974.

"Good heavens, *now* you tell me!
How lucky he is."

"You could join him," I suggest.

"I didn't like him *that* much," she replies.

Brief fling in the dementia ward

My mother has a brief flirtation
with Mr Otto, a rare male in Frail Care.
He has the look of a Slavic conductor
– sweeping, side-parted silver locks
offset his visible nappy line.

"How odd," Ma says of Mr Otto,
"to meet the love of one's life in a kitchen"
and to him, within hearing of the nurses:
"Your place or mine?"

But then, just as quickly, she forgets him
and Mr Otto wanders the passageways again,
asking if anyone has seen his wife;
it's not like Mrs Otto to be home so late.

Butter

You know how it is sometimes with butter?
How after a free fallow period, you long for it,
how it lies shaded in its pale soft firmness,
how it calls to you quietly from its cool clay dish

until at last you give in, you make toast:
you don't even want the toast –
burnt crumbs mean nothing to you –
but you but you but you want the butter.

Well, that's how it was with you.
I'm saying this in as plain a sliced way as I can –
there may after all be children present:
you were any old slice of toast.

I can't be more explicit than this;
I can't slick this on any thinner.
You may have thought you were the butter
but you weren't: you were the toast.

How I knew it wasn't me

I only realised I was at risk
when my brother phoned to check if I was still alive –

he'd heard it on the radio:
a woman fitting my description apparently wept
on the harbour wall before she dived.

    "So it wasn't you?"
a query rising in his tone.

I too – as I replied – couldn't help sounding
        unconvinced
as if searching for stronger proof.

After verbally confirming my existence,
I walked to the bay window and considered
the breakwater, the beacon
        the beckoning sea
and the woman who jumped in my place.

Summarising life

Summarising life is not easy.
My first try went like this:
You're born,
you go to the dentist,
then you die.

But that didn't quite capture all the pain,
so I tried again:
You're born,
you take your car to the mechanic,
then you die.

I was getting warmer,
I was definitely in the right room;
I just didn't know which cupboard life was in.

That's when I looked out of the window:
the full moon ran across the bay towards me
and Paderewski played Chopin on the TV.

So I wrote:
You're born, you hear the Polonaise héroique;
you forget the dentist and the mechanic,
then you die.

No, not quite. Try, try, try:

You die. You go to the dentist.
You take your car to the mechanic.
You look out of the window.

The full moon runs towards you across the sea.
Paderewski brings his hands down on the keys.

You're born; you start crying.
Eventually, you do die.

But the only part you're conscious of
– the only part that stays –
is the Polonaise.

To the doctor who treated the raped baby
and who felt such despair

I just wanted to say on behalf of us all
that on the night in question
there was a light on in the hall
for a nervous little sleeper
and when the bleeding baby was admitted to your care
faraway a Karoo shepherd crooned a ramkietjie lullaby in the veld
and while you staunched
there was space on a mother-warmed sheet
for a night walker
and when you administered an infant-sized opiate
there were luxuriant dark nipples
for fist-clenching babes
and when you called for more blood
a bleary-eyed uncle got up to make a feed
and while you stitched
there was another chapter of a favourite story
and while you cleaned

213

a grandpa's thin legs walked up and down for a colicky crier
and when finally you stood exhausted at the end of her cot
and asked, "Where is God?",
a father sat watch.
And for the rest of us, we all slept in trust
that you would do what you did,
that you could do what you did.
We slept in trust that you lived.

Petra Müller

Intensive care, thoracic ward

Heat has bleached the colour from the roses
in the smallish garden outside.
Inside, now, the cancerous oesophagus is gone.

Disappeared from the body – the thing which sounds
like an important lost play from the Greek. He lies
strung by wires and loops, a sailor subject fit for contemplation
like odysseus writ small. Pain is his doorway and his craft:
opened from the sternum down, repeated
in the red slash at the back.

Many voices are heard in his blood. They trace their curves
on paper scrolls: the mother who survived the holocaust,
the father who saw Berlin burn; even the wife, here,
contemplating past and that which cannot yet
be called a future.

The journey is extensive and not done. Gods in white coats pass
and rustle. They discuss the traveller lashed to the mast
of his black boat, yearning, yearning
for the music of the shore. He must sleep,
not entertain these fitful dreams.
They put their fingers to their lips
and watch him enter quiet waves.

Enormous procedures take place off-stage. And are noted –
some requiring black ink, others move into the red.
Tenacity skips up, skips down, is criss-crossed by *tonos*:
ah, the tone of things! We always enter music at the end.

Opera is work, work becomes the opera, the thing done
well at last when closest to the bone – a life lived
to the point of sheer obliteration,

walled wildly by the garden outside
where the noon sun now has blanched all colour
from the stunned and silent flowers.

Night crossing II

The old man has a wizened face
that suits the half-light of this riverplace;
his boat is rude, one half still rough with bark.
I hope it finds the other shore.
He treads the bobbing water, carelessly as people do
whose legs have found the proper way of balancing upon
the rim of water and of air. It is not far, and after
earthquakes upstream, shallower than it had been before.
Where *did* you find his name, in times like this,
and such a smooth address, like water folding
in upon itself. It sounds familiar enough.
The restless reeds are here called *schilf*,
this is the *schilfensee*. Remember when you reach
the other shore to call out once. But not my name –
a sound, it does not matter much, a nightjar, anything.

Do not attempt to speak his language: it will set
his teeth on edge. The fare is small,
a little something of the marketplace.
I pay. Do not hark back.

This time you go –

I stay.

TONI STUART

Ma, I'm coming home

Ma,
I'm coming home
the mountain that hangs
blue over our town
is calling me;
its voice
speaks soft in my ears
and the song of the southeaster roars
in my empty stomach

Ma,
I'm coming home
my heart is full of longings
and tears like stones
pour down my cheeks
lie hard and heavy on my chest
make it hard to breathe

the skin of my feet is torn
from walking
other distant
paths other people's
pain

I miss the sea
and the smell of salt
at our front door
in the summer morning
swollen by the heat

I miss the tongues and the speech
of my people
and their voices
that fall flat on words

the blood in my veins
beats to a rhythm
I can't find here in this green land

Ma,
I'm coming home
the mountain that hangs
blue over our town
is calling me
in the dark hours of the night
its voice
speaks soft in my ears
and the song of the southeaster roars
in my empty stomach

Ma,
I'm coming home
the time for the wide world is over
and I want to lie again
by
your side

Translated from the Afrikaans by Mike Dickman.

MARLENE VAN NIEKERK

Rock painting

Whoever set you upright here, little quagga foal,
alone on your first legs, a birth moment
no bigger than a hand, wobbly and with lips
parted in fresh bleating, eyeless
in the first light, a mouth tentatively
seeking the udder, whoever posited you here,
Equuleus of the Cederberg, in the first raising
of the rear, in the precarious tensing
of the forequarters, has flung a red balance into the grey
one-way grain of rock, fashioned a gravity
of defencelessness that concatenates us, tourists
of oblivion, in emotion, compassion,
courage, connects us to your first painter
in the unspectacular patriotism of tenderness.
In our navel stirs the same brush, red ochre, eland fat,
in our sight the same dead stars,
we who over the ages emerge from the brown river,
noticing and renaming you, preserve you forever, Celeris,
swiftly vibrating shadow on this liminal rock –
no matter whether you perish, your snout smashed
against the leaden law of the mightier,
or gambol away on lanky legs, lovely, prancing,
in the wine-brown water of time.

Winter finch

The small red finch
so deftly slips
from the swaddling
and unseeing snow
that all envelops,
and buries all,
he thrills
and puffs
his buff red bib,
flicks his tail,
turns the lanterns
on his wings, left
right, left,
preens the gold
fleck on his
pope and
aims
his beak
with an inspired eye
t'wards the ash's
knobbly buds,
vibrates
his craw
as if an ember
sets his throat
ablush –

and –

from the frozen holly,
snow divested
he escapes,

221

zips a zigzag trail of fire
across
the sky before
he fades,
a tint,
a sound,
that we tell each other,
and withhold,
and re-narrate
under the table lamp
when everything
has turned once more
to white and black
and silence
as before.

night psalm

it's a honky tonk that illumines the night
it's the keyboard of a honky tonk
down at the feet of things
at the feet of the lampposts
at the acrid feet of the olive trees
it's a metronome
at the sweeter feet of the lemongrove
at the vlei's little slippers of water
down at the bottom of the reeds
where the lilies lilt on stilettos
it's a rickety old honky tonk
maybe a loom

the spool and the shuttle
of a cranky old loom
or a smithy's tinker and tilt
down in the sump of the night
or a sewing machine with a tapping heel
that jig-jigs yonder in the quag
it's cheeky jazz on bell tongues
it's in the hoof of every culm
sans a tune
without amen
it's a honky tonk
it's a clapper key
it's a speckling under the dewclaw
it echoes from under the lavender
they're foot spoons
they're foot raps
of crickets and of toads
they're the ones that are a-tappin' and a-tickin'
unceasing in the mottle of the grass
to this I hum
to this I strum
to this I swingle
my night psalm

Translated from the Afrikaans by Marlene van Niekerk.

JIM PASCUAL AGUSTIN

Chameleon caress

With veins pulsing she grips
the branch that holds her up.
Tongue bunched inside
her jaws, soundless. Her slit
of flesh finally blossoms.

A ball of slime drops but refuses
to plunge to rough ground.
Membrane clings to closest
branch. In a breath, a limb
breaks that soft, transparent sheet.

And this thing, a minuscule version
of its mother, starts to climb. Born
with the same slumbering
acrobatic agility, it creeps upward,
seeks warmth for its fragile skin.

While she gives birth to another
and another. Until all life
nearly drained, she heads down.
Slow body gently presses
against each offspring,

a first and last caress.

Missed fortune

I will continue to set before you little bowls of colours
bright and pure if possible,
for what is needed in misfortune is a little order and beauty
– Czeslaw Milosz, "My Faithful Mother Tongue"

You are slowly turning into a stranger.
I speak and you look away, gaze
at passing trains, the blur
of writing on the sides of trucks,
swirl of pigeons in the sky.

I speak and your doubts grow thick
as traffic fumes on the palms
of beggars curled up in slumber.

You cannot trust someone
like me. You think I have abandoned
all the words I inherited,
exchanged them not even for riches
but for the life of a hermit.

I mumble to myself even when no one
is around. I dare not say
a word of you in crowds
for I am alien enough at first glance.

But you are wrong and easily offended.
I am patiently parting thick grass,
breaking down old doors.
The blood in my hands
is as warm as yours.

225

Bear with me and my misfortune.
My path may yet
lead me back home
laden with little bowls
brimming with colours
you have never seen before.

People who live with lions

Mandela would never live here. This suburb
was only on paper 17 years ago, the country
still intoxicated with ideas of freedom
and equality. It was once a vineyard. Farm workers
who lived in shacks without toilets

came down long narrow paths
to pick the darkening globes
by hand, their skin like bruised
banana peel. The week marked
by a salary of coins and alcohol.
Right here, where two lions

painted white sit on pedestals of bricks
on either side of the gated driveway,
there used to be a huddle of low trees
all the way to where the automatic
garage door nearly touches the ground.

Now it doesn't matter whether blacks,
whites, coloureds or some other shade
of skin park here: the lions stare
with eyes dull as cast cement.
This is where the workers used to pee.

Khadija Tracey Heeger

I am

I am the clue laid in mortar
a print of things gone and things to come
I am the blood of Aushumato, Sara Baartman, Eva Krotoa, Lydia...
I am the blood of Modjaji, Masbiker, Tjimba, Tambatu, the Igbo, the
Samburu, the Borana, the Akan, the Ewe, Tamil, the Pribumi, the
Dutch, the Huguenot, the British, the Indo, the Malay...
I am the string singing wordy mansions to the sky
I am the herb that heals.
I am the passion sinew that holds the vein of humanity tight so we
will always remember
I am the fighter spitting in the face of dilution
those castles that would kill the power of meaning
I am the spring of mixtures percolated in a myriad legions
The pageantry of a parentage that came from there and there
and there and there and there...
I am the confusion inside
I am that sneaky mess that dooms the science of purity
and casts a light on the wicked eye of narrow definitions that choke
my family
Your eyes will find me almost anywhere and when you do your heart
will not compare this
I am that thing...that thing you say "shame, no authenticity, no clan."
I am that thing that no tongue could name and no face could claim

I am the sound in your mouth as it fills with click and cursor
There I sit on the tip of your denial in the unmade bed of a South
Africa that slowed itself to constriction beyond apartheid and
fashioned its identity on that broken chain of history

I am the tide in you that may just drown those attitudes you hold so dear
about who is this and who is that and who will be counted in officialdom
I am the frown on your face as you point and slander "malaw!"
Ingratiating yourself with words like "black like me but not like you."
A slur on the name of freedoms bought in corridors of clinched deals

I am the precious pandora
The language of a Chaos we must all walk through
I am a trust broken down brick by brick in the thick of the possibility
of a Rainbow
a truth, a door
Proud Coloured!
Better still a proud Human!

On this giant plateau of experience, this steep curve
we will learn this one that intrudes on the construction of failed identity
My bones creak with the wakening of something, undefined as yet
A proof that we are all so much more than this
soon, very soon
don't blink
I am your skin
I am the living thing within
I am you.

Witness

And when they come to ask me who these people are
the ones whose roots run fibrous and convoluted beneath the surface
these people whose histories fall untidy onto pages
these people whose histories fall off pages out of memory into ectoplasm
these people bristling a self hatred in comedic caricature
I will say your name and your name and yours
I will say your name so loud the earth will split her tidy lips and the sky
    will fracture her seams
I will scream you up into each crevice so blush of you falls on all that is
    breathing, on all that is holy
I will say he was here, and she was here and he was here and she was here
I will take my sinewy tongue and spell your true names on the rapture of
    my skin
I will write you a proud voice in the mouths of babes, on the walls of caves
I will name your presence, your births, your deaths, your desires
I will play it out across the arteries of time
I will make you a monument beyond wood or stone
when they come to ask me who these people are
I will say: These are my people
your people
all people
in one people
this is my blood narrative to you.

Home

I have to draw maps.
I have to ride my feet like chariots.
I have to speak like stone and rock.
I have to see like water.
I have to love like mother tongue.
I have to wrestle with the bones of my dead.
I have to wade through the sands, leap through the dungeons
so I feel,
so I feel as I wonder through my life
not knowing me, not knowing now.
See my mirrors and my footprints dance,
me my back to the wind posing in the cracks of my winded smile.
See my questions barren, black shoving marks against these walls,
burning holes in charcoal dreams.
I am here but seldom seen.
I am here,
I am.

I have to draw maps.
I have to ride my feet like chariots.
I have to speak like stone and rock.
I have to see like water.
I have to love like mother tongue.
I have to wrestle with the bones of my dead.
I have to wade through the sands, leap through the dungeons
so I know,
so I know the dust-stamp footfall,
a murmuring earth call,
knowing where, knowing how
knowing me, knowing now.

I have to draw maps
to make the swindler mute
to sound the horn
to speak by using my own tongue and annihilate the mutant words.

I have to ride my feet like chariots
to win her back
to find her soles and grow my own
in the new places I call home.

I have to wrestle with the bones of my dead
so I may live here in their stead
carrying their wisdom on the lean road
learning the lessons by which I am led.

I have to wade through the sands,
leap through the dungeons
to find her footprint, to find her footprint
to make a footprint
to make a footprint of my own
so I will know
that I am
home.

DAVID WA MAAHLAMELA

Autobiography

after Nazim Hikmet

I was born in 1984
in a village not shown
on the map of my country.

at ten my parents divorced,
I quickly learnt to wear long pants,
slept at the orphanage and police station,
slept with street kids on cardboards,
survived bottomless gorges of misery.

poetry ambushed me at fourteen
though I did not know how to worship it
in the way it demanded.

at sixteen I matriculated,
E symbol as my highest,
confirming my teachers' curse,
your skull roofs a large room
that has no furniture
a year later I fought with lizards for sunrays
while my friends were in university.

I was a peddler and a gardener
before I allowed de beers and anglo platinum
to mine minerals with my nails,
a small torch of resistance showered my eyes,

I organised a protest march,
resigned so as to save others' jobs,
none was prepared to save mine.

death came for me three times,
my ancestors told it: go to hell!
piety possessed me
after my everything was repossessed,
I learnt to pray in hair-bristling caves,
bathe in sacred waterfalls
and hold talks with mountains,
only one mountain answered me.

I have been loved forever so many times,
but all my forevers have ended before the end.
I have never cast a vote in my life,
never believed in voting against, rather for,
I refuse to be anyone's spanner or hammer;
I enjoy biting the hand that feeds me
especially when it feeds me poison.

people say I'm lucky
not knowing the wars my roots fought
for every drop of water.

mine is a cast-iron heart
annealed by the furnace of turmoil and turbulence,
I have seen the unseen,
grown a third ear to hear the unsaid,
learnt to make love to gales.

NATHAN TRANTRAAL

Hammie

Dis poem I wrote twice
when my ma read da firs one
she say: "You can't write all dat stuff
dey gonna throw me in jail."

It's by her I learnt
howta hustle.
Not dat gangster-hustle
but dat woman-alone-lookin-out-fer-six-kids hustle,
dat righteous hustle.

My ma teach me
not to be sentimental.
Firs ting she pawned
was her weddin ring.

My ma greets gangster and church people da same
cos she knew da church people
befo dey become gangster
anna gangster befo
dey give dey heart to da Lord.
My ma don respek no-one too much or too little.

She smokes three packs a fags a day if she got em
an if she don, she picks up stompies
an roll us little fags wit da phonebook.
When you haven smoked all day
every puff feels like a man-sized hit.

My ma don believe in nutting an she believe in everyting
an you never know if she's lying.
She taught me how to lie
an how to tella story
an how to worry:
the secret is you go t'sleep.

You worry better when you rested.

Valhalla Park

There's grownups what sits onna pavement
an swear an curse an play dominoes;
babies what swear an curse
an play inna middle a da road
so da cars mus go round em;
whole famlies sittin by da street
in fronta dey houses an dey eyeball you
when you walk by.

There's geese inna road,
a hunnerd stray dogs,
a tousand stray people
an if you check dey faces
you can see dey all
dead a tousand years –
da people,
da geese
anna dogs.

Dey happy to be dere
an everyone what live in Valhalla Park
will tell you: Issa safest place if you live here
an I blieve em cos issa proven fact
dat da dead don haunt each other.

parable

My pa sit one night wit us
an tell us summin fucken weird.
He shows us when he was young
him an his brothers
went to steal figs inna Monte Vista.
Where da figs was, was mosly bush n sand
but dere was whitefolks houses closeby
wit fruittrees inna yard.

Den it happen dat da boere chase dem –
actually da boere's lighties –
wit sjamboks an stuff like at.
But what happen is, my pa an his brothers
like catch one of da white lighties inna bush
an kidnap him.

When dey got him alone,
dey pull him down onna groun
an one-by-one take a turn
an shit in his mouf.

Dats da story, da story of how my pa
took a dump inna white kids mouf.
Dats my pa's modest contribution
inna struggle against Apartheid.

I dunno if issa parable
or a true story –
da parable of da disgusting cunts?

I dunno how I feel bout dis story.
I dunno what hurt more:
if someone hit you wit a sjambok
or if someone take a shit in your mouf
an wipe his arse with your blonde hair

Fifa 06

Jake Donahue: *This is for Molly, this is for Prang, this for my brother,*
and this for the life you stole from me, you bastard!
– Keith W. Strandberg, *The King of the Kickboxers*

My pa sits inna car, pissdrunk
twelve of his best friends wit him.
Da car is shit small
an half da pricks a hangin out.
My pa is acting like a cunt.

My ma is standin by the frondoor
getting ready fo the fight wit him.
I stop by my ma, look around:

238

my pa is busy opening da gates.
He picks up a half a brick
an for two seconds I think
he gonna trow it at my ma.

But he toss it out the way
so he won have to ride over it.
Now I'm standing there watchin my pa
anna hypothetical situation
where my pa takes a brick an trows me with it
starts to play in my head.

Won be da firs time
he attacks me
an I think I still owe him for da time
he chased me an André wit a axe.
My ma tells him he can't come in here
but he's piss drunk an comes an stands
an swears at my ma an I'm just getting madder.

I push my pa over the low wall
so he falls on his back.
I climb over calm like and begin kicking him inna head.
I'm just completely fucked up mad
anna whole time I'm yelling at the man:
stop fuckin wit me, you fuckin fuck,
stop always fuckin wit me.

The way I'm kicking my pa is very Fifa 06,
it feels a bit fake an unconvincing
as if I'm jus going through da motions.

My ma is screaming like a madwoman for me to stop.
I stop cos da screamin makes me tired.

I look... my pa's not movin
an my ma's still screamin:
"I always tell you not to hit!"
My ma is cryin an I just want her to shut up.
I check my pa's dead
cos he's not doin nothin –
jus lyin there like someone showin off.
Someone drags me into da house, maybe my brother.
I check my pa's dead
but I don worry, I'm not afraid.

I think to myself
jail is like a rite of passage if you coloured:
one way or the other you gonna sit for summin.
Fuck all to do with who or what you are.
It's like a fuckin pilgrimage,
like da Muslims goin to Mecca.

I feel like someone who jus comin there now,
someone who dunno what's goin on,
cos everyone stands aroun my pa.
Then my sister's boyfrien comes in
an he gimme da same smile
he give when I say summin funny,
almos like he thinks me an my pa
was busy makin jokes.

But I trust Wanie's smile
cos Wanie is the best
at jumping on people's heads.
He jus laughs expertly and tell me
not to worry,
my pa's gonna wake up in thirty seconds.

He gives this whole scientific explanation
about my pa's blood alcohol levels.
I'm not listenin anymore,
cos I'm feelin low –
not about my pa,
I'd kick him to death a hunnerd times
if I could get away with it.
But it's that soun my ma makes
when she loses her nerve.

Translated from the Afrikaans by Mike Dickman.

Ronelda Kamfer

Where I stand

I'm sitting at table now
with my forefathers' enemies
I nod and say hello
but
deep inside me somewhere
I know where I stand

My heart and head are open
and we laugh and eat together
like well-brought-up folks
but
deep inside me somewhere
I know where I stand

Pick n Pa

I know all kindsa pa's

    pa's what don't work
    pa's what jus' hang out
    pa's in Pollsmore
    pa's what lies inna gutters
    pa's what sleeps inna day an' works inna night

I know all kindsa pa's

pa's what hates their kids
pa's what likes their daughters
pa's what hits their wives
pa's what gets sick with no wine
pa's what speak only sometimes

I know all kindsa pa's

except the one
I never seen

good girls

good girls don't join gangs
they don't get pregnant at thirteen
they don't have gang-tag tattoos
don't smoke weed
don't do crystal meth
don't have sex with teachers
or joll with taxi drivers
they don't work for Shoprite
they aren't cleaners
good girls don't live on the Cape Flats

Shaun

I can taste the fear, gonna lift me up and take me out of here
— Arcade Fire, "Intervention"

1.

you were little you said
you seriously
can't remember details
different people remember
different versions
of the same stories
your pa stepped in
somewhere
grabbed your ma by the arm
pushed her against the wall and
klapped her with the back of his hand
you're not sure which hand
it was
you remember each one of
the different times
you remember the klap because
your pa's name was also Shaun
and your ma screamed Shaun
you wanted to jump up and
go help
but
you weren't sure which Shaun
she was calling

2.

people say druggies could help themself
if they wanted
people say the problem is the drugs
but my friend Shaun doesn't believe
what people say anymore
he says if one day someone comes to him
and tells him how it feels to be 6 years
old and sleep under subway by Wynberg station
he'll maybe lissen
Shaun says if someone comes and tells him
how they lay down in front of Kentucky and slept
jus' to kinda be near food he might possibly lissen

Shaun is fuckin clever for someone
who only did five years school
he knows everything about everything
one day he recited f' me
like the park birds he came early
like the water he sat down

now that's jus po'try
he always said

Shaun was locked up for one or other
drug-related charge
shortly before his release he sent me
a letter to say when
he was coming out
and how he was now maybe ready to try
summing dif'rent

jail's no place for a person
was his last line
the day before his release
Shaun was murdered
people say it was drug-related narcotics this time
but I don't believe what people say anymore

dust

the charge office stank of dust
the lady who brought me's car also stank of it –
dust
the head's office
the social worker with the sweaty hands
the presbytery
the sickroom at the reformatory
all stank of dust
but the charge office dust was different
it stank like a dust what had had kids
and they'd all died
the cop who's job is just to do the charges
didn't look me in the eyes
he told me I could ask him anything
so I asked him what did he think of dust?
dust?
yes, dust, I caught his eye
he looked straight at me and said
that he didn't really think of dust
I told him I think of dust all the time
what dust is everywhere what dust knows great secrets

what sometimes I look for dust and I know dust has a smell
what dust means death and I wished I was dust

I told him dust can't go back to dust
but people can
ja, said he quickly,
shows you how worthless they are

him who never thinks of dust

retelling 2

a woman lived here Mad Maria she walked with a long rope round her
neck with her housekeys on one night she died with the keys round
her neck the wind broke her neck

you Cape people say the sun sees everything
here it's the people who see everything

i'm not crying over that Apartheid kak i'm crying that you kids only
hear about District 6 i can still smell the St Helena in my granma's hair
but brownfolks are always just mealy-mouthed stupid assholes being
brown is nothing to do with that bullshit story those muslims made up
and then it's the other story again about being bushmen the problem is
when you know your people's story and there's no muslim
or bushman in it but you just have to yes and amen because
all you've got is the retelling

the sea haunts you even when you move right into the desert

the sea's a bitch with red shoes on

Beware depression

If you been attacked
raped, hijacked, kidnapped, held prisoner
better make sure
you see a psychiatrist
all that stuff can depress you
is good reason for depression

shit folks
shit teachers
shit churches
shit food
shit people
shit clothes
shit rules
shit laws
shit music
shit weather
shit timing
shit poets
and a shit mood
are not causes for depression

They're just part of life

Translated from the Afrikaans by Mike Dickman.

Katharine Kilalea

Portrait of our death

There were four of us, following a dirt road which began
in the foothills and went right up into the mountains
where a little cottage was waiting for us. We were driving
slowly, packed in a blue hatchback, and it was getting late

and the rain, which had started earlier, had begun to really
pelt down. And then, coming round a sharp corner, we lost
our grip, the wheels skidded, wrestling with the thick
white rain, the mud.

The driver, my friend, said "whoa" like you'd say to a horse,
and lifted his hands from the wheel. And I remember
as the car began to spin the mountains turned green,
and as it edged slowly towards the end of the road,

we leaned in, as you do in films with a car at the edge of a cliff,
watching through the windows, mesmerised, as the valley opened up
in a passionate, open-mouth kiss. We should just have tumbled in,
but instead were left unfallen, not yet dead, with the radio still playing.

The driver, my friend, looked green. Our Death was not (as we'd
imagined) the blue car descending the steep gorge-without-ladder,
slipping like a dangerous dress-strap or a crap hand of cards
flung down in disgust. We'd stopped too soon,

left still as rocks, as upturned beetles wriggling their legs,
or the roadside cows chewing slowly. The driver, my friend,
lit a cigarette and sat down. The rain looked on with big cow-eyes.
Not-dying is suddenly being very hungry

and your wet brown shoes caked in mud but not caring
and the mountains feeling slow and the heavy grey clouds
like a washerwoman sprinkling cotton before ironing it flat.
Our Death was pure mathematics –

the steep angle of the cliff which didn't meet the speed of the car –
Our Death was a thing measured in increments, about 66% death
and 33% not-death (just a bit deathy). Probably, we decided,
the mosquitoes in this heat would've sucked us dry

before our death got to us anyway. It was just a slip of the wheels,
we said, a skid, perhaps we'd made too much of its nearness.
Our Death was just a minor character, someone who appeared
about ten miles after a town called River-Without-End, then went on.

And we felt quite energetic after that. It was hot. It was exciting,
what didn't happen that afternoon. We went hiking
and found a waterfall and fell from it
into deep black pools, lying underneath.

Portrait of the beach

New Year's Day. The sea smells of beer.
A helicopter is looking for sharks.
Two men are setting up a kosher hotdog stand
and it smells really terrible.

Two fat ladies in sunhats are walking very fast.
It's a little bit lonely. It's too early for swimmers
and a Grampa gets wet only to his ankles.
There are no lifeguards yet

but gradually, people come. We sit
facing the sea like in a cinema.
Two lifeguards arrive and erect two flags
to mark the swimmable waters.

I twitch to dislodge flies. I swim
in the shallows and see a sand-shark
till a wave comes and mushes everything around.
The sea seems very small.

My resolution is to forget the things I say
when I am drunk. The cold water makes me feel better.
A wave pulls off my bikini bottom
and a current pulls me in deeper.

We laze in the water like dishes in the kitchen sink.
A couple is playing bat and ball.
A girl in a bikini is posing for her boyfriend
and I don't have it in me

not to look. An old woman rubs her husband's back
with a red towel
then his shoulders
then his old, wet arms.

I am reading Ted Hughes again
and he says, "On this evening
nothing could make me think I would ever be needed
by anybody". I am a wild creature.

My eyes are red from salt,
skin wrinkly from the sea –
my hair, sticky, and starting to separate from itself
as it dries.

A young man looks at the sea, and at me,
with big dog-eyes
and then leaves. Identical twins arrive,
very thin, like two halves of one person.

I think the sea is soft like a dog
which has got a duck
and brought it to the side of the lake
still alive in its mouth.

A perfect love

You are a tortoise in a hard hat.
I am a heart growing gallons and gallons of hair.

You made it with me: a perfect love,
which went hard from the softness of its innards.

And though all the love went elsewhere, you hung around,
like a gas, like sand in my bikini pants.

Hennecker's Ditch

I stood at the station
like the pages of a book
whose words suddenly start to swim.

Wow. The rain. Rose beetles.

Formal lines of broad-leaved
deciduous trees
ran the length of the platform.

Ickira trecketre stedenthal, said the train.
Slow down please, said the road.

Sometimes you get lucky, said the estate agent
onto his mobile phone,
it all depends on the seller.

Dear Circus,
Past the thicket, through the window,
the painéd months are coming for us –
See the bluff, the headland
announcing the presence of water.
See the moths...

The trees walk backwards into the dark.

*

Hello? Hello? The snow comes in sobs.
Dogs sob.
Cars sob across town.

Dear Circus,
When you found me I was a rickety house.

There was a yellow light and a blanket
folded up on the stoep
and the yellow light
Dear Circus
was a night-blooming flower.

We pushed a chest of drawers
against the door.
It's nice now that the corridor's empty.
A necklace. Vacant. Light wrecked the road.

Dear Circus,
We took off our clothes
and did cocaine for three weeks.
The washing machine shook so badly
that a man asleep four floors down
reached out to hold it:
Shut that dirty little mouth of yours.

*

Hennecker's Ditch.

You'll never find it, he said over dinner,
a black lobster and bottle of vinegar,
unless, unless...

Blackened, the dog tilts his head
from beneath the canopy of the Karoo tree.
Look at my face, he said. Can you see what I'm thinking?

A red jersey. Bot bot bot. Sevéral breezes.
Boats on the water were moving at different speeds.
The baker took a portable radio into the garden
to listen to the cricket in the shade
of the bougainvillea.
Tick-a-tick-ooh, tick-a-tick-ah.
We were moving as shadows.

Three times he came upstairs and made love to her
then went back down and read his book.
The air was blood temperature
and the consistency of blood.

Look at my face, he said.
I see you. I see you. I see you in our murky bath
I see you in our black and white bath
like a cat.

*

Barbed wire around the fisheries.
A letter from the municipality
Come closer, sir. Step into my office.

Above the harbour, tin roofs and cranes.
Henry? he said. Hello? Henry? he said.
What's been happening in Dog Town these days?
The Audi keys lay heavy on the table.
Ah Henry, he said. How wonderful it is to see you.

The mists came down. The moon was bright.
Collectors searched the night market
with flashlights, and the wind outside,

with its slight chill, howled.
Henry, the breezes – they bolt across the open market
like meatballs, Henry, like windmills, Henry,
like policemen, Henry, apprehending criminals.

A man in a collared shirt put a cigarette to his mouth
and looked at his watch.
And what happened then?
He wore a street hat. He wore a street hat
and carried a belt over one arm.
And what happened afterwards?

Tell her... I think he has given up.
Tell her...

He closed the door and came in.
He closed the door and the sound of the bathwater dimmed.

*

Thirty-one back gardens.
Thirty-one back gardens overlooking
the backs of thirty-one houses.
Thirty-one houses looking out over the sea.
And the sea, of course it was, was marbled
and contorting.

Are you sleeping? Yes.
Figures in yellow mackintoshes make their way
along the coastal path.
And what then, what if I were to ask, How much longer?
If I were to say, How much further?
It's just

I have used up all my reserves.

There was a yellow light
and a blanket folded up on the stoep.
The light was burning dimly now.
By that time,
the light had begun to flicker.

He opened the door and fastened his lonely shadow,
and she fastened hers and sat on the chair.

I think we are in the middle, aren't we.
He said, I think we may be.
We certainly aren't at the beginning anymore.

*

The moon was acting strangely.
The moon was moving fast.
It was cloudy but hot.
Electricity cables gathered round a pole
like the roof of a marquee.

He wore a gold vagina on his chest.
He had gold lining on the flaps of his jackét.
She lay her head against the window and sang a song
by Silvio Rodriguéz
wearing ten gold balls on a chain around her neck.
Dear Circus,
Sometimes we are just so full of emotion.

And what happened then?
And what happened afterwards?

Chicken bones and Pick 'n Pay receipts.
We were moving as shadows.
And the only light
was the light from the bakery.

A lampshade swings above the window.
Tick-a-tick-ooh, tick-a-tick-ah
We have no history.
Nothing has passed between us.
A hundred years pass like this.

Dear Circus,
I need to see more glass!
I need to see more glass!
This has to be more gentle.

NOTES ON SOME POEMS

These notes mainly concern some poems in which language other than English are used, and certain quotes whose sources are not mentioned in the poems themselves. In the case of Vonani Bila and Joan Metelerkamp, notes were provided by the poets themselves when their poems were originally published.

pp. 57-59 "In the name of Amandla" by Vonani Bila

Mqombothi (Nguni) traditional beer with a malt, corn and yeast base.

Mbhawula (Xitsonga) brazier.

Malahla (Nguni) coal.

pp. 60-74 "Ancestral wealth" by Vonani Bila

I

Kenya A woven grass mat used to roof huts. Among the Vatsonga, this mat was also used to wrap and preserve the corpse of a poor person who couldn't afford a decent blanket or linen.

Xihlungwani A carved wooden crown that is used to close the top of a grass-thatched hut. Among the Vatsonga, when the head of a family dies, the xihlungwani is removed to indicate that he is no more; and the place is usually referred to as emachihweni (see below).

II

Garankuwa One of ten Bantustans created by the apartheid regime.

Dzelehani (Xitsonga) bushbaby. A tiny nocturnal animal with a cry like a human baby, usually considered a bad omen.

III

Mhani (Xitsonga) Mom.

Mbhokota A populated rural village near Elim in Limpopo province.

N'wana wa munhu u le kusuhani (Xitsonga) The Son of Man is nearby, meaning Jesus is coming.

Emachihweni (Xitsonga) A deserted place usually occasioned by the passing of the head of a family. This metaphor implies that when the head of the family dies, there is a strong possibility of lawlessness, hunger, starvation, cheating and immorality in the family.

Emathumbhanini (Xitsonga) A children's makeshift abode of reeds or cardboard or other scraps, usually used for early sexual experimentation.

Mapfalo ya mina a ma file (Xitsonga) I had no regret (for having wanted to commit suicide).

IV

Vho (Xitsonga) Added to a person's name as a title of respect, e.g. Mr. or Mrs.

Emaxubini (Xitsonga) In the ruins.

V

Hahani (Xitsonga) Aunt.

Muhulu (Xitsonga) Your mother's sister.

A ka ha ri vusiku (Xitsonga) I was in the dark, meaning: I wasn't yet involved with girls.

Ku fanele ku songiwa masangu (Xitsonga) Proverb meaning: Mats must be folded. In other words, all sexual relations are prohibited.

Ta lava hundzeke emisaveni (Xitsonga) For the deceased. The name of a regular programme on radio Tsonga in the 1980s.

Eka (Xitsonga) Preposition 'at'.

Wa (Xitsonga) Preposition 'of', shorthand for 'son of'.

Xi nga ri na nhonga xi sila hi mandla (Xitsonga) He who crushes [tobacco] without a mortar and pestle but with bare hands.

Sivara (Xitsonga) Brother-in-law.

Mokhukhu (Sepedi) Shack dwelling. In this poem, this word refers to the Zion Christian Church's organised, rhythmic, male dance which is characterised by frequent and collective leaps into the air and coming down stamping their feet on the ground with their white boots called manyanyatha. Usually, the mokhukhu performances last for hours, with no meals in between, except the drinking of sugarless tea and mogabolo (holy and blessed water) before the performance. The mokhukhu dancers are usually called mashole a thapelo, meaning the soldiers of prayer.

VII

Madala (Nguni) Old man

7/8 u ya lithanda isaka la mazambani/ U ya lithanda isaka la mazambani An IsiZulu song particularly liked by the poet's father. The composer is not known, but the song was performed by a male song and dance troupe during his father's school days at Shirley Agricultural and Industrial School for Natives, and during the potato tasting festivities organised by the Swiss missionary and liberal Herbert Stanley Phillips and his wife Lucette Phillips, at Shirley farm.

Vaveni (Xitsonga) Tokoloshe, evil spirit or voodoo.

And hi yena buti wa Frank (Nguni) And he's the one who is Frank's uncle.

pp. 114-115 "Nonhlanhla" by Isabella Motadinyane

Bayavuya umoya wami (Nguni) They are happy.

Uyakathazeka (Nguni) My soul is troubled.

p.157 "Kingdom of Rain" by Rustum Kozain

Die Kleurlingkant is vol (Afrikaans) The side for Coloureds is full.

p.165 "That river, that river" by Rustum Kozain

Juffrou is ook hier (Afrikaans) Miss (the female teacher) is also here.

pp. 191-201 lines quoted in "Points on poems" by Joan Metelerkamp

"No ideas but in things": William Carlos Williams, "Paterson".

"Happy, happy": John Keats, "Ode on a Grecian Urn".

"The energy that's divine": Angifi Dladla, "Song of the fertility doll".

"The still point of the turning world": TS Eliot, "Little Gidding".

"Sixthly and lastly": William Shakespeare, Dogberry the constable in *Much Ado About Nothing*.

"Not the apotheosis but the pattern": Louise Glück, "Ripe peach".

"Affirmation of the affirmation": Gilles Deleuze on Nietzsche in *Pure Immanence*.

Robert Duncan, Scales of the Marvelous: title of a book on his work subtitled *Working papers in contemporary criticism*.

"The activity of perception or sensation in Greek is aesthesis which means at root 'taking in' and 'breathing in' – a 'gasp', that primary response": James Hillman, *The Heart's Thought*.

Biographical Notes on Poets and Translators

Jim Pascual Agustin: Born in Manila, in the Philippines, in 1969, he grew up under the dictatorship of President Marcos. He did literary studies at Ateneo de Manila University. In 1994 he immigrated to South Africa, and now lives in Cape Town where he works as a translator and writer. He has published six books of poems, two in Filipino, two in English, two of them containing poems originally written in both languages.

"Chameleon caress" was published in *Alien to Any Skin*, Manila, University of Santo Tomas Publishing House, 2011. "Missed fortune" was published in *Sound Before Water*, Manila, University of Santo Tomas Publishing House, 2013. "People who live with lions" appears in *New Coin*, Vol. 49, N°1, June 2013.

Gabeba Baderoon: Born in 1969 in Port Elizabeth, she grew up in Cape Town and studied at Cape Town University as well as the University of Sheffield, specializing in the question of the representations of Islam in South African media and culture. She moves between South Africa and the United States, where she lectures at Penn State University. She has published four books of poetry.

"True", "Where nothing was" and "Cinnamon" were published in *The Dream in the Next Body*, Cape Town, Kwela Books/ Snailpress, 2005. "Postscript" appears in *The Museum of Ordinary Life*, Stuttgart, Daimler, 2005. "Fit", "I forget to look at her", "The pen" appear in *A Hundred Silences*, Cape Town, Kwela Books/ Snailpress, 2006.

Robert Berold was born in Johannesburg in 1948. He studied chemical engineering at the University of the Witwatersrand, economics and English at Cambridge. He has worked in NGOs with small homestead farmers and handcraft producers, and has also worked as a freelance technical editor. He is the publisher of Deep South, a small press specialising in South African poetry, and for ten years was editor of the poetry magazine *New Coin*. Besides his four collections of poetry, he has published an anthology of South African poetry, a book of interviews with South African poets, a widely distributed manual for small farmers, a biography, and a memoir of a year in China. He coordinates the MA programme in Creative Writing at Rhodes University.

"Angel" was published in *Rain Across a Paper Field*, Pietermaritzburg, Gecko/UKZN Press, 1999. "To my room", "The water running", "All the days", "The rock thrushes", "Letter to Mary" and "Visit to my mother" are taken from *All the Days*, Grahamstown, Deep South, 2008.

Vonani Bila was born in 1972 in Shirley village, Limpopo, and studied at Tivumbeni College of Education. His father was an amateur musician, his mother a historian and storyteller. A poet and musician himself, he is founding editor of the *Timbila* poetry review, publisher of Timbila books and founder of Timbila Writers' Village, a writers' residence in a rural context. He recently graduated with an MA in Creative Writing from Rhodes University. He has written eight story-books for newly literate adult readers in Sepedi, Xitsonga and English, the latter two being the languages in which he writes poetry. He was the editor of *New Coin* poetry journal in 2013. He has brought out a CD of his poetry and music, as well as four volumes of poetry.

"In the name of Amandla" appears in *In the Name of Amandla*, Elim, Timbila Poetry, 2004. "Baba Mandela" appears in *Handsome Jita*, Durban, University of KwaZulu Natal Press, 2007. "Ancestral wealth" and "The toilet cleaner at OR Tambo International Airport" are taken from *Tyhini*, journal of students of the Masters programme in Creative Writing at Rhodes University, 2012.

Jeremy Cronin was born in Durban in 1949 and spent his early childhood in Simonstown. He studied at Cape Town University, and then at the Sorbonne in Paris, obtaining a Masters degree in philosophy. He lectured in philosophy and political science at the University of Cape Town, but his activities in the South African Communist Party and links with the African National Congress led to his arrest in 1976, followed by seven years in prison. On his release he became editor of the United Democratic Front journal *Isizwe* (The Nation) and worked in the field of popular education until police harassment forced him into exile. He was appointed Deputy Minister of Transport in 2009, and has been Deputy Minister of Public Works since 2012. He is the author of countless political articles, and has published four collections of poems.

"End of the century – which is why wipers" was published in *More than a Casual Contact*, Cape Town, Umuzi, 2006.

Ingrid de Kok was born in 1951 in Johannesburg, and grew up in the gold mining town of Stilfontein. She specialized in literature and politics at the University of the Witwatersrand, Johannesburg and the University of Cape Town, doing further studies in Canada where she lived for seven years. She will shortly retire from the Centre for Extra-Mural Studies at the University of Cape Town, where she designs and coordinated adult education, liberal arts and capacity building projects, national colloquia and cultural programmes.

She has published six volumes of poetry.

"Stay here", "Notes for that week" and "What kind of man?" appear in *Seasonal Fires*, Cape Town, Umuzi, 2006. "Married late", "My muse is a man", "Meeting after much time has passed" and "Histoplasmosis: a guide's instructions at the cave" are taken from *Other Signs*, Cape Town, Kwela Books/ Snailpress, 2011.

Mike Dickman was born in Johannesburg in 1947. His formal academic studies include George Boyes Art School, the University of Cape Town and INALCO, in Paris where he lives. More significant to him have been studies done under Tibetan Buddhist teachers. Most of his early career was spent as a musician; he has made four recordings of his songs, as well as publishing a book of poems, *The Edge*. He is a practitioner and teacher of Yang-style taiji quan, and also works as a translator of Tibetan and other spiritual texts. In addition to translating some of the poets in this anthology, he has also completed an unpublished manuscript in English of Adam Small's *Kitaar my Kruis*.

Isobel Dixon was born in 1969 in Mthatha, where her father was Dean of the Cathedral, and grew up in Graaff-Reinet, in the Karoo. She studied English literature at the University of Stellenbosch and then at Edinburgh University before settling in Cambridge, England, and starting work as a literary agent in London, representing many South African writers among others. She has published three collections of poems.

"The skinning", "Tear", "After grief" and "Back in the benighted kingdom" are all taken from *A Fold in the Map*, Cambridge, Salt Publishing, 2007 and Johannesburg, Jacana Media, 2007.

Finuala Dowling: Born in 1962 in Cape Town to two well-known radio broadcasters, she studied English literature at the University of Cape Town before lecturing in English at the University of South Africa. She now lives in Kalk Bay and works as a freelance educational materials developer, writer and lecturer. She has published three novels and three volumes of poetry.

"To the doctor who treated the raped baby and who felt such despair" appears in *I Flying*, Cape Town, Carapace, 2002. "At eighty-five, my mother's mind", "How I knew it wasn't me", "Widowhood in the dementia ward", "Brief fling in the dementia ward", "Summarizing life" and "Butter" are all taken from *Notes from the Dementia Ward*, Cape Town, Kwela Books/ Snailpress, 2008.

Khadija Tracey Heeger was born in Cape Town in 1966, raised on the Cape Flats in the township of Hanover Park, and studied Museum and Heritage issues at the University of the Western Cape. She is a facilitator with the Scalabrini Centre, running cultural cohesion workshops in schools. She also works as a performance poet and is a member of the Cape Cultural Collective, an inter-generational, multi-racial organisation that provides a platform for emerging artists while using the arts to celebrate culture and history. She has published one collection of poems.

"Home" was published in *Beyond the Delivery Room*, Cape Town, Modjaji Books, 2013. "I am" and "Witness" are previously unpublished.

Denis Hirson: Born in 1951 in Cambridge, England, he lived till the age of 22 in Johannesburg where he studied Social Anthropology at the University of the Witwatersrand, later obtaining a doctorate in Creative Writing at the University of East Anglia. In 1975 he settled in France, where he lives near Paris. He has worked as an actor, does readings of South African poetry with an actress and saxophone player, and teaches English at the École Polytechnique. One of his seven books is a history of South African writing since the nineteenth century, another a volume of poetry. He has also produced three anthologies of South African poetry in French and an anthology in English covering the period 1960 - 1996.

"Time Lines" is in *We Walk Straight So You Better Get out the Way*, Johannesburg, Jacana Media, 2005. "Scar" and "Initiation" are taken from *Gardening in the Dark*, Johannesburg, Jacana Media, 2007. "Why dogs would make good writers" was first published in the *Poetry Salzburg Review* No. 22, Autumn 2012. "Cider and water", "Doctor fish" and "The song of the crows" are previously unpublished.

Richard Jurgens was born in 1960 in Johannesburg. He studied philosophy at the University of the Witwatersrand. After a short spell in publishing he went into exile in various countries in Africa and Europe, amongst other things working with the ANC, before returning to South Africa in 1994. Presently, he divides his time between Johannesburg and Amsterdam, working as a writer, editor and translator. In 2004 he co-founded *Amsterdam Weekly*, an alternative cultural newspaper. He has published a memoir, *The Many Houses of Exile*, and a book of poetry, *One Summer*. His first novel, *The Incident on Heron Island*, is due out in 2014.

Ronelda Kamfer was born in 1981 in Blackheath, outside Cape Town. She was brought up by her grandparents, both of them farm workers, before being sent back to her parents in Eersterivier, on the Cape Flats. After matriculating in 1999 she worked as a waitress and clerk, then as a nurse while writing her first book. She later studied Afrikaans, Dutch language and literature at the University of the Western Cape under Antjie Krog, and currently works as a freelance editor. She has published two volumes of poems and is currently completing her third volume, along with a novel and a graphic novel.

"Where I stand" (Waar ek staan), "Pick n Pa", "good girls" (goie meisies), "dust" (stof) and "Beware depression" (Pasop vir depressie) appear in *Noudat slapende honde*, Cape Town, Kwela Boeke, 2008. "Shaun" and "retelling 2" (oorvertel 2) appear in *grond/ Santekraam*, Cape Town, Kwela Boeke, 2011. Mike Dickman's translations have not been previously published.

Keorapetse Kgositsile: Born in Johannesburg in 1938, he went into exile in the United States from 1962 to 1975. A founding member of the ANC's Department of Arts and Culture and that of Education, he was Chairperson of the Regional Political Committee in Zimbabwe, and worked in Botswana in the underground structures of the Political/Military Council (PMC). He also studied literature and creative writing at Columbia University, later teaching at a number of universities including the University of Denver, Wayne State University, UCLA, and the universities of Dar es Salaam, Nairobi, Botswana, Zimbabwe, Zambia and Fort Hare. He was one of the first poets to bridge the gap between African and Afro-American poetry, doing readings in New York jazz clubs. In 1990 a book of his was published in South Africa for the first time. He has lived in Johannesburg since 2001, was elected National Poet Laureate in 2006, and works as special advisor to the Minister of Arts and Culture. He has published nine books of poems and a book on the art of writing poetry.

"Affirmation" and "Renaissance" are taken from *If I Could Sing*, Cape Town, Kwela Books/ Snailpress, 2002. "No Boundaries" appears in *Beyond Words*, Great Britain, Defeye, 2009.

Katharine Kilalea: Born in South Africa in 1982, she studied at the University of Cape Town, and left for England in 2005. She obtained a Masters degree in Creative Writing from the University of East Anglia, and is currently studying for a PhD in Creative Writing at the University of Sheffield. She represented

South Africa at the London Southbank Centre's Poetry Parnassus in 2012, and has published one collection of poems.

"Portrait of our death", "Portrait of the beach" and "A perfect love" are taken from *One Eye'd Leigh*, Manchester, Carcanet, 2009. "Hennecker's Ditch" is published in the *New Poetries V* anthology, Manchester, Carcanet, 2011.

Rustum Kozain was born in Paarl in 1966. He studied English literature at the University of Cape Town and creative writing at Bowling Green State University, Ohio, before lecturing in Literature, Cinema and Popular Culture at the University of Cape Town until 2004. Since then he has worked as a freelance editor and writer, living in Cape Town. He has produced anthologies of short stories and poems used in South African high schools and colleges, and has published two volumes of poems.

"Kingdom of rain", "Leaving" and "Stars of stone" are taken from *This Carting Life*, Cape Town, Kwela Books/ Snailpress, 2005. "That river, that river" and "Death" appear in *Groundwork*, Cape Town, Kwela Books/ Snailpress, 2012. "Dear comrades" appeared in *The Big Issue* (Cape Town), December 2012. "Memory 1" is previously unpublished.

Antjie Krog was born in Kroonstad in 1952 to a family of writers. She did literary studies in English and Afrikaans at the University of the Orange Free State and the University of Pretoria. She has worked as a teacher, editor and radio journalist, covering the Truth and Reconciliation Commission. Her three books of non-fiction deal with this Commission, the transformation process in South Africa, and African philosophy. She has also co-authored a book about TRC testimonies with Professor Kopano Ratele and Nosisi Mpolweni. She is currently Professor at the University of the Western Cape and lives in Cape Town. She has also written a play, three children's books and twelve books of poetry in Afrikaans. Three collections of her poetry have been published in English.

"Country of grief and grace" (Land van genade en verdriet) and "Poet becoming" (Digter vordende) are from *Kleur Kom nie Alleen nie*, Cape Town, Kwela Boeke, 2000. "Arrival" (Liedere vir die pasaangekomenes), "morning tea" (oggendtee), "how do you say this" (hoe sê mens dit), "Sonnet of the hot flushes" (sonnet van die warm goede) and "Winter" appear in *Verweerskrif*, Cape Town, Umuzi, 2006. Antjie Krog's translations into English (sometimes in slightly altered form) are all taken from *Skinned*, New York, Seven Stories, and Umuzi, Cape Town, 2013.

David **wa Maahlamela** was born in 1984 in Mankweng, Limpopo. A qualified fitter and turner, he worked in the mining industry for almost a decade before becoming a full-time writer. He recently completed an MA in Creative Writing at Rhodes University. He is the author of a novel, a play, and six children's books, all written in Sepedi. He has also published a volume of poetry in Sepedi, and is currently compiling an anthology of Sepedi poets.

"Autobiography" was published in *New Coin*, Vol. 49 N°1, June 2013.

Sindiwe Magona was born in Gungululu in the Transkei in 1943 and grew up in a township near Cape Town, working as a domestic servant while completing her secondary education. She later graduated from both the University of South Africa and Columbia University. She has worked at the United Nations as a civil servant, and has also been a motivational speaker, actor, Xhosa teacher and translator. Writing in both Xhosa and English, she has produced over a hundred children's books, three plays, two books of short stories, autobiography, novels, radio plays and a screenplay.

Bongekile Joyce Mbanjwa was born at KwaNxamalala in Pietermaritzburg in 1962. She studied at the University of Natal, KwaZulu-Natal Sign Language Academy and UNISA. She has worked for the Natal Society for the Blind and Epilepsy SA as a social auxiliary worker, at Endumezulu Adult Centre as a teacher and at UNISA as a tutor. She has published one bilingual volume of poetry, *Izinhlungu Zomphefumulo* (Emotional pain), in Zulu with English translations by Siphiwe ka Ngwenya.

"Lock and key" (Isihluthulelo) and "Why?" (Kanti kungani) were published in the anthology *Isis*, ed. Allan Kolski Horwitz, Johannesburg, Botsotso, 2005, in Zulu with English translations by Siphiwe ka Ngwenya.

Joan Metelerkamp: Born in Pretoria in 1956, she grew up on a farm in Natal. After studying drama at the University of Natal she worked in the field of educational drama. She has since taught at the University of the Western Cape, the University of Natal, and at Rhodes University in the Masters programme in Creative Writing. From 2000 to 2003 she edited the poetry journal *New Coin*. She lives in Knysna, and has published eight volumes of poems.

"Deliver her from the depths" is taken from *requiem*, Grahamstown, Deep South, 2003. "Intact" and "Points on poems" appear in *Burnt Offering*, Cape Town, Modjaji Books, 2009.

271

Kobus Moolman was born in 1964 in Pietermaritzburg, where he still lives. He teaches creative writing in the English Department at the University of KwaZulu-Natal, Durban. He was the editor of the literary journal *Fidelities* from 1995 to 2007, and has edited an anthology of creative work by South African writers living with disabilities. He has published two collections of radio plays and six collections of poetry.

"Two moons" was published in *Light and After*, Grahamstown, Deep South, 2010. "*They come again*" was published in *Left Over*, Sandton, Dye Hard Press, 2013. "From a Canadian diary" first appeared online at http://incwadi.wordpress.com/

Isabella Motadinyane was born in 1963 in Soweto, where she was brought up by her grandmother. After five years of primary education she studied piano, dance and theatre in Johannesburg before writing and performing poetry in several languages, including Sotho, isicamtho and English, in particular with the Botsotso Jesters, of which she was a founding member. She was also part of the Botsotso Publishing venture. She died in 2003, on her fortieth birthday. A book of her poems was published posthumously. Translations from isicamtho and Sotho are by Ike Mboneni Muila.

"Nonhlanhla is gone", "Red crown", "Come people" and "Sink a shaft" all appear in *Bella*, Johannesburg, Botsotso Publishing, 2007.

Ike Mboneni Muila was born in Soweto in 1957, grew up in Venda, Limpopo and now lives in Mofolo. He worked in theatre before he began writing poetry. He has published widely in literary magazines, and performed his isicamtho poetry at many festivals in South Africa as well as Europe. He is a founding member of Botsotso Jesters performance group and the Botsotso Publishing editorial board. He has published one book of poems, drawings and voice recordings, titled *Gova*.

Petra Müller was born in 1935 in the small enclave of Botrivier, where her father was the village policeman. She spent some of her childhood on a farm outside Swellendam. After studying at Stellenbosch University, she worked as a fiction editor and features writer for *Sarie* magazine, then as a publishing editor and later as a freelance journalist. She lives in Cape Town. A fully bilingual writer in Afrikaans and English, she has published seven novels (five using the nom de plume Magriet Smalberger), five collections of short stories, three children's books and seven collections of poems, all of them in Afrikaans apart from the last one, *Night Crossing*, written in English.

"Intensive care, thoracic ward" and "Night crossing II" were both originally written in English and published in *Night Crossing*, Cape Town, Tafelberg, 2006.

Gert Vlok Nel was born in 1963 in Beaufort West, Western Cape, where his father worked for the South African Railways. He studied English, Afrikaans and history at the University of Stellenbosch and worked as a tourist guide, barman and guard before settling in the village of Gouda in the Karoo and working as a musician, performing regularly in South Africa and the Netherlands. He is the author of two collections of poems, and has produced two CDs of poems and songs, all of them in Afrikaans with the occasional use of English.

"leaving behind the beautiful words of Beaufort West" (om Beaufort-Wes se beautiful woorde te verlaat), "Beautiful in Beaufort West" (Beautiful in Beaufort Wes), "Hillside lullaby" and "Why I'm calling you tonight" (Waarom ek roep na jou vanaand) were first published in *Om Beaufort-Wes se Beautiful Woorde te Verlaat*, Cape Town, Quiellerie, 1999. "River" (Rivier) and "Epitaph" are on the CD *Beaufort-Wes se Beautiful Woorde*, Munich Records, 2006. The translations by Richard Jurgens appear on the Poetry International website http://www.poetryinternationalweb.net/pi/site/poet/item/428. The translation by Mike Dickman is previously unpublished.

Siphiwe ka Ngwenya was born in 1964 in Soweto, where he still lives. He has a diploma in speech and drama from Fuba Academy, and has worked as both a theatre director and organizer of poetry readings. As a writer he has been a member of AWA and COSAW, and a founder member of the Botsotso Jesters. He has published a volume of poetry, *Soulfire Experience*, and has performed his work widely.

Mxolisi Nyezwa was born in 1967 in the township of New Brighton, outside Port Elizabeth, where he still lives, earning a living by running a skills training project for unemployed young people from a converted steel container in Motherwell township. He is the founding editor of the English/Xhosa cultural magazine *Kotaz*, and teaches in the MA in Creative Writing programme at Rhodes University. He has published three volumes of poems.

"It all begins" is in *Song Trials*, Pietermaritzburg, Gecko/UKZN Press, 2002. "Story", "Songs from the earth", "Letters of demand", "The road ahead", "*They have asked me many times*" and "*How do I say this, that once your eyes*" are taken from *Malikhanye*, Grahamstown, Deep South, 2011.

JC (Koos) Oosthuysen was born of missionary parents in 1933 in Port St Johns, Eastern Cape. He learned to read and write in the isiXhosa medium mission school at Isilimela, later studying Philosophy at the University of Stellenbosch, Theology at Yale University and African Languages at Rhodes University. He served as minister of religion in the Uniting Reformed Church and was seconded for 20 years to the Bible Society of South Africa. He has written a graded grammar of isiXhosa, *Leer Self Xhosa*, and translated the hymnal *Hosana*, *The Lion Children's Bible* and *Twintig Verse in Vertaling* as well as co-ordinating work on the 1996 isiXhosa Bible. He has just completed an unpublished book of isiXhosa grammar, extricating it from the constraints of a Eurocentric approach, as well as a comprehensive graded grammar of isiXhosa in both English and Afrikaans.

Karen Press: Born in Cape Town in 1956, a writer and freelance editor, she has produced textbooks for the teaching of science, mathematics, economics and English. In 1987, she co-founded the publishing collective Buchu Books, and later helped set up a national advice and information support service for South African writers, The Writers' Network. She has published stories for children, books for newly literate adults and a film scenario, and is a translator into English of the work of Antjie Krog. She has published nine volumes of poems.

"Glass cabinet – the watch" is taken from *The Little Museum of Working Life*, Pietermaritzburg, University of KwaZulu Natal Press, 2004. "Walking songs for Africans abroad" is in *The Canary's Songbook*, Manchester, Carcanet, 2005. "Do you love yourself like this", "Pasternak's shadow", "Praise poem: I saw you coming towards me" (extract) and "A cow and a goose" are all in *Slowly, As If*, Manchester, Carcanet, 2012.

Mongane Wally Serote was born in 1944 in Sophiatown and grew up in Alexandra township just outside Johannesburg. Engaged in the Black Consciousness movement, he was detained in 1969 and spent nine months in solitary confinement. In 1974 he went into exile in the United States, studied at Columbia University and then in Botswana in 1977 where he joined Mkhonto we Sizwe. There he also co-founded the Medu Art Ensemble, an association of artists in exile. Seven years later, he began working for the Department of Arts and Culture of the exiled ANC in London. Returning to South Africa in 1990, he became head of the ANC's Department for Arts and

Culture, and was later elected to parliament. Until recently, he was head of the Freedom Park Trust in Pretoria, and is now CEO of iARi, an organisation which promotes the concept of African Renaissance on the basis of indigenous knowledge. He also works as a sangoma, a traditional healer. He has published a book of essays, five novels and ten volumes of poems.

"Freedom, lament and song" is an extract of the long poem *Freedom Lament and Song*, Cape Town, David Philip, 1998.

Ari Sitas was born in 1952 in Limassol, Cyprus, where he grew up, later coming to Johannesburg where he studied sociology and philosophy at the University of the Witwatersrand. He was one of the founding members of the Junction Avenue Theatre Company. In 1983, involved in trade union work in Durban, he helped develop popular culture, founding a workers' theatre and publishing a book of worker poetry, *Black Mamba Rising*. A professor of the Department of Sociology at the University of Cape Town since 2009, he has recently worked on the ethics of reconciliation, both in South Africa and Cyprus. Apart from numerous sociological works, he has published seven volumes of poetry.

The six extracts from "Slave trades" are part of *Slave Trades & An Artist's Notebook*, Grahamstown, Deep South, 2000.

Kelwyn Sole: Born in 1951, he studied at the University of the Witwatersrand and the School of African and Oriental Studies, London. He worked as a teacher and administrator in Botswana and also in South West Africa, from which he was expelled in 1980 under the Undesirable Aliens Act. He was briefly co-editor of the literary review *Donga*, before it was banned by the apartheid regime. A Professor of English at the University of Cape Town, where he has worked since 1987, he is also a literary critic specializing in questions of South African and postcolonial literature and culture, and has written numerous essays on South African poetry as well as editing a selection of contemporary South African poetry for the American journal *The Common*. He has published six volumes of poems.

"To be inside" appears in *Love That is Night* Pietermarizburg, Gecko/UKZN 1998. "This is not autumn" and "The land" are taken from *Mirror and Water Gazing*, Pietermaritzburg, Gecko/UKZN, 2001. "I never meant to cross the river", "I live in a house" and "He had to come in" appear in *Land Dreaming: Prose Poems*,

Pietermaritzburg, University of KwaZulu-Natal Press, 2006. "New country" is in *Absent Tongues*, Cape Town, Modjaji/Hands-On Books, 2012.

Rosamund Stanford was born in 1956. She grew up on a farm in East Griqualand, and studied literature and politics at the University of Cape Town. She works as a freelance writer, editor and project manager, most recently for Rhodes University, where she produced a manual on southern African heritage management. She has written television comedy scripts and short fiction stories for educational purposes, and has published two volumes of poems.

"Forefathers" and "Ditch" are in *The Hurricurrent*, Grahamstown, Deep South, 2011. "Our president" was published in *New Coin*, Vol 49 No2, December 2013.

Toni Stuart was born in Cape Town in 1983 and has a National Diploma in Journalism from the Cape Peninsula University of Technology. She co-founded the NGO "I Am Somebody!" which uses storytelling and youth development to build integrated communities. She is a member of the Cape Cultural Collective, an inter-generational, multi-racial organisation that provides a platform for emerging artists while using the arts to celebrate culture and history. She is also curator of Poetica, organizing poetry events at Cape Town's Open Book festival. Her work has previously been published in various anthologies.

Mike Dickman's English translation of "Ma ek ko huis toe" (Ma, I'm comin' home) is previously unpublished. The original poem has appeared online as an audio recording on the Badalisha Poetry Radio, http://badilishapoetry.com/radio/toni-stuart/ An English transliteration of the poem accompanies the audio track.

Nathan Trantraal was born in 1983 on the Cape Flats, where he grew up. A self-taught artist, he works as a professional cartoonist, collaborating with his older brother as The Trantraal Brothers. They have created a serialized comic series for the *Cape Argus*, brought out two comic albums and a weekly cartoon strip for the *Cape Times* called *The Richenbaums*. Nathan Trantraal has brought out one volume of poems in Afrikaans.

"Hammie", "Valhalla Park", "parable" (gelykenis) and "Fifa 06" all appear in *Chokers en Survivors*, Cape Town, Kwela Boeke, 2013. The translations by Mike Dickman are previously unpublished.

Marlene van Niekerk was born in 1954 in Caledon in the Western Cape. She studied languages, literature and philosophy at Stellenbosch University, then philosophy and cultural anthropology at Amsterdam University. She was also a directing apprentice for a time, in theatres in Mainz and Stuttgart, Germany. She has taught philosophy, Afrikaans and Dutch literature in several universities, and is currently Professor at the department of Afrikaans and Dutch at Stellenbosch University, and has also done teaching stints at the Universities of Utrecht and Leyden in the Netherlands. She has published three novels, two volumes of short stories and three volumes of poems, all originally in Afrikaans.

"Rock painting" (Rotstekening), "Winter finch" (Wintervink) and "night psalm" (nagpsalm) all appear at http://www.poetryinternationalweb.net/pi/site/poet/item/23457, the Poetry International website, in Marlene van Niekerk's English translations. The original Afrikaans poems appear in *Kaar*, Cape Town, Human & Rousseau, 2013.

Bulelani Zantsi was born in Cala, Eastern Cape, in 1976. His maternal grandfather was a chief of the Thembu clan. He worked as a shepherd and garage attendant before attending the University of the Western Cape, where he studied geography, psychology and Xhosa and obtained a teaching diploma. Since 2001 he has been a high school teacher specialized in the teaching of classical Xhosa, and has also worked as a radio broadcaster. He discovered his vocation as an imbongi at university, and has participated in numerous official occasions including opening a session of parliament and honouring personalities such Archbishop Tutu and Thabo Mbeki when he was president.

"Clan names of the AmaBhele" and "Praise-singers of the house of Ntu" have not been previously published either in Xhosa or in this translation, which is by Sindiwe Magona, JC (Koos) Oosthuysen and Antjie Krog.

Acknowledgements

For permission to use previously published work in this volume, grateful acknowledgement is made to the following: *New Coin*, the University of Santo Tomas Publishing House and the author for poems by Jim Pascual Agustin; Daimler, Kwela Books, Snailpress and the author for poems by Gabeba Baderoon; Deep South, Gecko Books/ the University of KwaZulu Natal Press and the author for poems by Robert Berold; Timbila Poetry, *Tyhini*, the University of KwaZulu Natal Press and the author for poems by Vonani Bila; Umuzi and the author for the poem by Jeremy Cronin; Kwela Books, Snailpress, Umuzi and the author for poems by Ingrid de Kok; Jacana Media, Salt Publishing and the author for poems by Isobel Dixon; Carapace, Kwela Books, Snailpress and the author for poems by Finuala Dowling; Modjaji Books and the author for poems by Khadija Tracey Heeger; Jacana Media, *Poetry Salzburg Review* and the author for poems by Denis Hirson; Kwela Boeke and the author for poems by Ronelda Kamfer, Mike Dickman for his translation's of Kamfer's "Where I stand", "Pick n Pa", "good girls", "dust", "Beware depression", "Shaun" and "retelling 2"; Defeye, Kwela Books, Snailpress and the author for poems by Keorapetse Kgositsile; Carcanet and the author for poems by Katharine Kilalea; Kwela Books, Snailpress, *The Big Issue* and the author for poems by Rustum Kozain; Kwela Boeke, Seven Stories, Umuzi and the author for poems by Antjie Krog; *New Coin* and the author for the poem by David wa Maahlamela; Botsotso Publishing and the author for poems by Bongekile Joyce Mbanjwa, Siphiwe ka Ngwenya for his translations of Mbanjwa's "Lock and key" and "Why?"; Deep South, Modjaji Books and the author for poems by Joan Metelerkamp; Deep South, Dye Hard Press, incwadi. wordpress.com and the author for poems by Kobus Moolman; Botsotso Publishing for poems by Isabella Motadinyane; Tafelberg for poems by Petra Müller; Quiellerie, Munich Records and the author for poems by Gert Vlok Nel, Mike Dickman for his translation of Nel's "leaving behind the beautiful words of Beaufort West", Poetry International and Richard Jurgens for his translations of Nel's "Beautiful in Beaufort

West", "Hillside lullaby", "Why I'm calling you tonight", "River" and "Epitaph"; Gecko Books/the University of KwaZulu Natal Press, Deep South and the author for poems by Mxolisi Nyezwa; Carcanet, the University of KwaZulu Natal Press and the author for poems by Karen Press; New Africa Books and the author for the poem by Mongane Wally Serote; Deep South and the author for the poems by Ari Sitas; Gecko Books/the University of KwaZulu Natal Press, Modjaji Books and the author for poems by Kelwyn Sole; Deep South, *New Coin* and the author for poems by Rosamund Stanford; Toni Stuart for "Ma, I'm comin' home", and Mike Dickman for his translation of it; Kwela Boeke and the author for poems by Nathan Trantraal, Mike Dickman for his translations of "Hammie", "Valhalla Park", "parable" and "Fifa 06"; Human & Rousseau and Poetry International for poems by Marlene van Niekerk; Bulelani Zantsi for "Clan names of the AmaBhele" and "Praise-singers of the house of Ntu", and Sindiwe Magona, JC (Koos) Oosthuysen and Antjie Krog for their translations of these poems into English.